Toxic Empathy

Toxic
Empathy

HOW PROGRESSIVES EXPLOIT
CHRISTIAN COMPASSION

Allie Beth Stuckey

SENTINEL

SENTINEL
An imprint of Penguin Random House LLC
penguinrandomhouse.com

Copyright © 2024 by Allie Beth Stuckey
Penguin Random House values and supports copyright. Copyright fuels
creativity, encourages diverse voices, promotes free speech, and creates
a vibrant culture. Thank you for buying an authorized edition of this book
and for complying with copyright laws by not reproducing, scanning, or
distributing any part of it in any form without permission. You are supporting
writers and allowing Penguin Random House to continue to publish books
for every reader. Please note that no part of this book may be used or
reproduced in any manner for the purpose of training artificial intelligence
technologies or systems.

SENTINEL and colophon are registered trademarks of Penguin Random House LLC.

Most Sentinel books are available at a discount when purchased in quantity
for sales promotions or corporate use. Special editions, which include
personalized covers, excerpts, and corporate imprints, can be created when
purchased in large quantities. For more information, please call (212) 572-2232
or email specialmarkets@penguinrandomhouse.com. Your local bookstore
can also assist with discounted bulk purchases using the Penguin Random House
corporate Business-to-Business program. For assistance in locating a participating
retailer, email B2B@penguinrandomhouse.com.

LIBRARY OF CONGRESS CATALOGING-IN-PUBLICATION DATA
Names: Stuckey, Allie Beth, author.
Title: Toxic empathy : how progressives exploit Christian compassion /
    Allie Beth Stuckey.
Description: New York : Sentinel, [2024] | Includes bibliographical references.
Identifiers: LCCN 2024027079 (print) | LCCN 2024027080 (ebook) |
    ISBN 9780593541944 (hardcover) | ISBN 9780593541968 (ebook)
Subjects: LCSH: Political culture—United States. |
    Christianity and politics—United States. | Christian ethics—
    Political aspects—United States. | Compassion—Religious aspects—Christianity. |
    Empathy—Political aspects. | United States—Politics and government—1989–
Classification: LCC JK1726 .S78 2024 (print) | LCC JK1726 (ebook) |
    DDC 306.0973—dc23/eng/20240716
LC record available at https://lccn.loc.gov/2024027079
LC ebook record available at https://lccn.loc.gov/2024027080

Printed in the United States of America
2nd Printing

For Mom and Dad, my original balcony people

Contents

Introduction

IT WAS LIKE I COULD feel her anxiety. I saw the stress in her body language, heard the unease in her voice, as she pleaded with her screaming baby to calm down. She was struggling down the jet bridge, shushing her few-month-old in his carrier while lugging multiple carry-ons and her folded-up Doona stroller onto the plane. "It's ridiculous American Airlines doesn't let families with small children board first," I thought for the hundredth time.

I was on a work trip alone, so I had a free hand. I closed the gap between us as we boarded the plane. "Can I help you carry something?" I asked. She looked back. "No, I'm fine." I would've said the same thing. I'm not really sure why. It's just reflexive to reject help—especially from strangers—even when we obviously need it. But I saw the tears brimming in her eyes, so I knew she hadn't meant her rejection. A few moments later, I insisted. "Let me carry the stroller. I'll follow you to your seat." She agreed. We got her and her baby settled, and she said thank you. I noticed she wasn't on the verge of tears anymore.

I'd been there—exactly there—just a few weeks earlier. I was going to Atlanta for a speaking engagement, and I was with my oldest, who was three and in the middle of her runaway era. This was the first time I'd traveled alone with one of my kids, so I was more stressed than usual. On top of that, I was dealing with one of those merciless gate agents who was completely uninterested in accommodating us.

Typically when traveling with babies, my husband and I had collapsed the stroller and left it at the top of the jet bridge for an airline employee to take down and stow away. So we stood there, ready to board and drop off the heavy contraption that I'd broken a sweat folding while wrangling my elusive toddler. Without looking up at me, the gate agent said I'd need to take it down the jet bridge myself. "I can't do that," I said. I didn't have enough hands to get everything and everyone onto the plane. She didn't offer a solution. She just told us to move out of the way while others boarded.

I shuffled us to the side as much as I could, and I sat on the ground with my restless daughter, who was determined to sprint down the jet bridge solo. I told myself not to cry because that wouldn't help. I got a few sympathetic looks as people stepped over and around us to get on their flight. Finally, a woman knelt down and asked, "Can I help you?" I wanted to say no. But I was about to lose it, fighting back tears. Considering how obviously desperate I was, I knew it would be ridiculous—and honestly inconsiderate to everyone in whose way we sat—to reject it. "Actually, yes," I said. Another woman behind her followed her cue and offered to carry my other bag. The one who first offered help said, "I'm a mom too. I've been there." I was thankful.

"I've been there." That changes everything, doesn't it? There was a time when I hadn't been there. Before I had kids, I'm embarrassed to say that when I heard babies screaming on planes or running around chaotically in airports I thought, "Why do parents travel with little kids?" Or "Just give them some Benadryl!" I laugh at myself now, realizing how little I understood then. I had no idea at the time that those parents feel a great deal more stress and frustration than I did at their child's behavior. I didn't consider that the child may be tired, scared, overwhelmed, or stressed herself. I had no concept of these things, because I hadn't been there.

You're more likely to understand someone's position—their perspective, feelings, and needs—when you experience what they've experienced. Even if you haven't lived through the same struggle, you can still try to imagine their pain and offer help. The ability to place yourself in another person's shoes—with or without having had a similar experience—is typically called "empathy."

By this definition, empathy is a powerful motivation to love those around you. It precludes unfair criticism and presumptuousness and motivates us to help people who need it. This kind of empathy can help us become better neighbors, friends, and parents, as we consider how to treat people the way we'd like to be treated. This isn't so different from Jesus's command to "Love your neighbor as yourself." Just as we naturally seek to meet our own needs, we should seek to meet the needs of others.

Some of the most memorable heroes in history have been those who were, in part, motivated by empathy. Corrie ten Boom, in her biography, *The Hiding Place*, recounts the intense compassion she and her family felt for the Jews fleeing from the Nazis. While they were moved by a Christian obligation to oppose injustice, it was their love for vulnerable Jews and their belief in their shared humanity that compelled them to hide Jewish people in their home. They saw and felt the pain of their Jewish neighbors and placed themselves in front of the target.

In a way, Jesus embodied empathy when he took on flesh, suffered the human experience, and bore the burden of our sins by enduring a gruesome death. Hebrews 4:15 describes Jesus as a great high priest who is able to empathize with our weaknesses, who was tempted in every way as we are, yet was without sin.

But empathy alone is a terrible guide. It may be part of what inspires us to do good, but it's just an emotion and, like all emotions, is highly susceptible to manipulation. That's exactly what's happening today. Empathy has been hijacked for the purpose of conforming well-intentioned people to particular political agendas. Specifically, it's been co-opted by the progressive wing of American society to convince people that the progressive position is exclusively the one of kindness and morality.

I call it toxic empathy.

Toxic Empathy

If you really care about women, you'll support their right to choose.
If you really respect people, you'll use preferred pronouns.
If you're really a kind person, you'll celebrate all love.
If you're really compassionate, you'll welcome the immigrant.
If you're really a Christian, you'll fight for social justice.

You're probably familiar with this line of thinking. The goal of statements like these—examples of toxic empathy—is to get us to suppress our opposition to a particular issue or point of view by playing upon our desire to be a good person.

No one wants to be seen as unempathetic, because a person who completely lacks empathy may be a narcissist. They're unable to see anyone else's point of view and refuse to bear their suffering. They're selfish and coldhearted. They ignore the struggling mom lugging her bags and her toddler down the crowded jet bridge.

That's why toxic empathy is so persuasive. It extorts a real and good desire that most people have, which is to be, and to be perceived as, kind.

But empathy and kindness are not synonymous, and neither are empathy and compassion. Kindness describes how we treat someone, either in word or deed. Compassion means to suffer with someone who's struggling. Both kindness and compassion are necessary components of love. But empathy literally means to *be in the feelings* of another person. Empathy by itself is neither loving nor kind; it's just an emotion. Love, on the other hand, is a conscious choice to seek good for another person.

The erroneous conflation of love and empathy has convinced the masses that to be loving, we must feel the same way they do. Toxic empathy says we must not only share their feelings, but affirm their feelings and choices as valid, justified, and good. This confusion has not only made us a morally lost people but it's also harmed the very people empathy-mongers claim they're trying to help: the truly marginalized and vulnerable.

Empathy for a desperate, pregnant woman may lead us to support her choice to have an abortion. But this empathy can blind us to the reality that abortion is a brutal procedure that kills a valuable person and leaves a woman with physical, emotional, and spiritual scars.

While empathy for someone who is deceived about their gender may lead us to affirm their stated identity, it is not possible to become the opposite sex, and this lie leads to policies that compound their deception and jeopardize the safety of women and children.

While empathy for a gay person may bid us to celebrate their lifestyle, redefining the family endangers children and can inhibit gay-identifying people from repenting and following Christ.

While empathy for the immigrant may tempt us to open our borders, that kind of immigration policy is dangerous both for America and for the people trying to come here.

Toxic empathy claims the only way to love racial minorities is to advance social justice, but "justice" that shows partiality to the poor or those perceived as oppressed only leads to societal chaos.

Empathy can help us see their perspective and foster compassion, but that's all it can do. It can't guide us into making the right decisions or donning the wise, moral, or biblical position. Toxic empathy bullies us into believing that the unwise, immoral, and unbiblical position is actually the righteous one.

I've found myself compelled by toxic empathy arguments on each of these issues at different points of my life. Like you, I want to be kind, and any accusation that I may lack empathy hurts. I've always had a heart for the underdog. I hate bullies. Because of that, I've had the propensity to be persuaded by emotional arguments from people claiming to be champions of the downcast. But as I've learned more about these subjects, I've realized how vital it is to push past superficial, feelings-based arguments and to pursue what is good, right, and true.

Christians are called to love, not just empathy. While empathy may help us love, it is not love itself. Empathy feels pain, but love always "rejoices with the truth" (1 Cor. 13:6). We must seek and speak the truth in love (Eph. 4:15). Because God is love and is the Source of truth, we can only embody this truth-and-love dichotomy to which we're commanded by defining both love and truth as He defines them (1 John 4:8). We look to His Word—not our feelings—as our guide in all things, including the hot-button cultural and political issues of our day.

As we'll see again and again, progressive positions are often—if not always—untruthful and unbiblical and are, therefore, also unloving. They sound good and often begin with good intentions, but they obscure the entire truth, convincing people to vote for policies—and embrace lifestyles—that are ultimately destructive.

To love means to want what is best for a person, as God defines "best." God's definition of what is good and loving will almost always contradict the world's definition, which will inevitably put us at odds with mainstream culture. While this is uncomfortable, the sacrifice is worth it. The truth can change lives.

I have the privilege of writing and speaking for a living. On my podcast, *Relatable*, where I analyze culture and politics through a biblical lens, I often hear from readers and listeners who tell me God used something said on the show to change their mind. One of these listeners is Daisy Strongin, a young woman who, as a teen, began "identifying" as a man. At age eighteen, she started on testosterone. She underwent a double mastectomy at age twenty. She soon realized that her dramatic transformation didn't give her the satisfaction and confidence for which she longed. By 2021, she'd detransitioned and become a Christian. In 2023, she messaged me on Instagram and told me *Relatable* played a major role in her acceptance of her God-given gender.

She first listened in 2019. "I originally started listening because I thought you were nutty, to be honest," her message read. "But then for some reason I kept listening and found that I was struggling to rebut you in my head." She didn't just wrestle with my arguments about gender; she also felt convicted by the theology-focused episodes as she struggled to reconcile her feelings with Christianity. Eventually, her mind and heart changed, and the Lord called her to repentance. She stopped denying her femininity and embraced her true gender, as well as her real identity as God's child.

Over the years, I've received thousands of similar messages—some about abortion, some about gender and sexuality, some about reproductive technology, and others about faith. Listeners and readers thought one thing and then were convinced of the opposing position either by things I said or by a point made by a guest on my show.

God gets the credit for changed hearts and minds, because He alone gives growth to the seeds planted by the truth spoken in love (1 Cor. 3:7). His Word never returns void; it will always accomplish what He wills (Isa. 55:11). That means when we tell the truth as He defines it, no matter how nervous we are or how uncomfortable it is, it will bear fruit in accordance with His perfect will. We may not see the immediate results of our obedience, but we can rest assured that God uses every lovingly truthful word spoken to bring Him glory and advance His Kingdom.

When you have a public platform, you field a lot of criticism. This criticism is amplified times a thousand when you wade into politics and religion. Because the issues I discuss—like abortion, gender, and immigration—are not only politically polarizing but personally sensitive, I receive plenty of angry messages. Some of them are downright evil and hateful, some are reasonable disagreements, and many others fall into the category of empathy manipulation. "If you had empathy, you'd take XYZ progressive position."

At times it gets to me, particularly when I'm met with the insistence that talking about an issue less or differently would win more people to Christ. The last thing I want to do is push people away from the biggest and best Truth: the saving gospel of Jesus. But then I think of Daisy. I think of the sonogram pictures from people who let me know they've decided to no longer put off having kids, and the baby pictures from the women who wanted to tell me they've chosen life instead of abortion. And I remember that God is faithful to use our truth-in-love efforts to make real change and save real lives.

If I could go back, I would change certain things I've said. There are times I should have been gentler or could have been more compelling. I've allowed my pride and frustration to get the best of me. I've either cared too much about people's feelings or not enough. Sometimes I've been ignorant to the truth and other times I've been too afraid to share it. Sometimes I've had way too much empathy and other times not enough.

While it's important to repent of sinful anger, ego, or fear, the gracious reality is that God doesn't need perfect messengers, just willing, prayerful ones. I can tell you from years of experience that softening the truth about an issue doesn't persuade people. Be kind, yes, but be clear and strong. Understand that, no matter how sweet you are, if you're saying something true or articulating a controversial perspective, there will always be critics telling you you're being too harsh and divisive. They'll demand, of course, that you have some empathy, which is typically code for: "You must agree with me."

And when they employ this tactic, you'll need to remind yourself that, perhaps completely unbeknownst to you, God is using your courageous obedience to accomplish His purpose.

For the Christian, empathy should never compel us to affirm that which God calls sinful or to advocate for policies that are ineffective at best and deadly at worst. While I could understand Daisy's sadness and distress that led to her "transition," truth-filled love urged me to talk about the fixed, biological male-female binary, knowing that embracing this reality is a better, healthier, biblical alternative to living a lie and mutilating the body. This approach is always worth risking hurt feelings.

The same principle can be applied to all of the most heated subjects of today: abortion, sexuality, immigration, and social justice.

This book isn't about killing empathy. It's about embracing God's vision for love, order, and goodness. My goal is to equip you with commonsense, biblical truths that dismantle toxic empathy from its foundations.

Again: real love—the kind described by the God who created and *is* love (1 John 4:8)—always includes truth. The two are inextricably intertwined, since true love celebrates truth (1 Cor. 13:6). Christians are called to this kind of love *regardless* of whether we feel empathy or not. Christians love because Christ first loved us, not because we feel a certain way or have had a particular experience (1 John 4:19).

That's why empathy is different from love and why it also must be *submissive* to love. Putting yourself in someone's shoes may help you feel their pain, but their pain isn't determinative of what's true or false, right or wrong. A person for whom you feel empathy may, in their pain, believe or demand things that are untrue, unhelpful, and even harmful. We can empathize with the pain of withdrawal for a drug addict, for example, but it would be cruel to give them the heroin they crave.

This tension between empathy and love is less relevant in most everyday interactions—like when you come across a struggling mom at the airport—and more intense when it comes to the politically charged issues of our day. In these circumstances, we often confuse the empathy that motivates us to help people around us with the empathy that's demanded of us by progressive activists.

Here's what I mean.

The Black Square and the Right Side of History

On the morning of June 2, 2020, I opened Instagram and started to scroll. My explore page looked different than usual. Instead of news updates, pregnancy announcements, and vacation photos, I saw one after the other blank, black squares. At first I thought it was a glitch. I clicked on a post, then another, then another. They were all accompanied with a similar caption: "Black lives matter." "Listening and learning." "In honor of George Floyd."

My own timeline looked similar, but with a more Christian flair. Captions read, "Made in the image of God." "You cannot love God and hate your brother." "One in Christ."

It wasn't difficult to see what was happening. Someone, somewhere, had started a movement to post all-black photos to mourn the death of George Floyd and to condemn the racism they claim enabled it. "Should I post too?" I wondered. "Of course I should. Right?"

People I respected—friends, pastors, authors, and influencers—were all joining in. These were thoughtful, sincere people, people who loved Jesus. Except for maybe the addition of a Bible verse in their caption, their posts were identical to those of the people who were not Christians, whose worldview is in stark contrast to my own. Maybe the fact that both sides were posting the same thing was a good sign. Maybe something was finally uniting us.

I thought some more about posting. It would've been easy to do. It would've been a way to demonstrate my empathy toward Floyd and victims of racism. A way to signal that I, too, denounce racism and was troubled by the now-viral clip of Officer Derek Chauvin pinning Floyd down with his knee. Both of these things were true, so why shouldn't I communicate that along with everyone else? Of course I think hating or mistreating someone because of their skin color is wrong. Of course I think police officers shouldn't use unnecessary force. Of course I believe all people are made in God's image and therefore possess an innate dignity that demands equal treatment and respect. If that's what the black square meant, then I was for it.

Just a few months earlier, a young black man named Ahmaud Arbery had been fatally shot in Georgia. While the circumstances leading up to his killing are still cloudy, we know he was running in a neighborhood when he was chased down and killed by three white men. Before discussing the incident on my show, I talked to one of my friends, who is black, to get her take on the situation. Expectedly, her reaction was characterized by sadness and some fear. While we didn't know the motivation, it wasn't hard to imagine that my black friends may have a unique perspective that I didn't, that they'd be troubled by the incident in a deeper way that I couldn't fully understand. But I could put myself in their shoes and do my best to imagine. I could allow myself to have empathy.

And now this. When I first saw the clip of Chauvin and Floyd on Twitter, my stomach dropped. My immediate response was, "What the heck? What is this? Why is this necessary?" It looked like undue force. Chauvin's face seemed to express apathy as he rendered helpless a person in pain, a grown man crying out for his mama. As a new mom myself, it felt like a gut punch. In the wake of Ahmaud Arbery, I knew the optics of a white officer pinning down a seemingly helpless black man was going to cause even more of a stir than usual.

I just didn't realize how much more. The reaction online was seismic and swift. While many shared my horror, the conversation on social media almost immediately graduated from "What's going on here?" and "This doesn't look good" to "We need systemic change" and "Abolish the police."

It was this shift that made me take a step back. I understood the sadness and even the anger, but I couldn't get down with the calls for revolution. I couldn't get on board with the transition from mourning what appeared to be inhumane treatment of a fellow image bearer of God to an indictment of America itself and police as a whole. Furthermore—and this was the thing most people were too scared to ask out loud—how did I know the situation had anything to do with race?

This last question made me even more uncomfortable with what I saw as I scrolled through the black squares on Instagram. Whether someone posted it with a Bible verse, "Justice for George Floyd," or "#BlackLivesMatter," they all seemed to be posting under the same assumption: that Floyd's death was the result of racism. Thousands of people of all ethnicities tragically die every day, many of them in unjust ways, and few, if any, receive social media attention. The death of George Floyd got a black square because of the belief that his death pointed to a bigger, deeper problem of racial discrimination in the United States.

And I just wasn't sure that was true. How could I know Derek Chauvin's heart? How could I know his motivations, whether or not he pinned Floyd down because of racial animus? That's essentially what these people were saying—that we can safely assume that because Chauvin was a white police officer and Floyd was black that Chauvin was a racist. And from this accusation followed the assertion that policing in the United States systemically discriminates against black people. Is that true? Is it correct to assert that America is still, today, plagued with pervasive, institutional racism?

I felt pressure to signal my own sympathy. Of course I believe black lives matter. But I knew from previous research that the organization Black Lives Matter, for which many black-square posters were soliciting donations, did not have goals I could get behind. They are open about their radical left-wing ideals. Now erased from BLM's website was this: "We disrupt the Western-prescribed nuclear family structure requirement by supporting each other as extended families and 'villages' that collectively care for one another."[1] While mothers and caregivers are named as members of these "villages," fathers never are. Cofounder Patrisse Cullors described herself as a "trained Marxist."[2] Among their list of stated demands is defunding law enforcement.

These are just a few examples of the group's far left radicalism. In addition to these ideals, they also offer a warped definition of justice that I couldn't get behind. And as a conservative and Christian, I'd never agree to uphold values I see as destructive. According to the

Bible, God's justice is, among other things, impartial (Leviticus 19:15). It doesn't show favoritism toward people because of their socioeconomic class, ethnicity, gender, etc. Black Lives Matter and those aligned with the organization seemed intent on indicting some people of racism and alleviating other people of responsibility based on the color of their skin.

But it felt verboten to say these things at the time. It was easier not to think about them, much easier not to voice them. In the wake of George Floyd's death, social media users were eager to prove their compassion and virtue. People posted their new summer reading lists, which included *White Fragility* by Robin DiAngelo and *How to Be an Antiracist* by Ibram X. Kendi. White people denounced their inherent privilege and announced their commitment to dismantling white supremacy. Christian leaders called for justice for black America, urging the church to see confronting systemic racism as a biblical mandate.

Carl Lentz, the then-lead pastor of Hillsong NYC, was active in the months after George Floyd's death in urging Christians to fight against systemic racism. "We need a new system," he wrote on Instagram. Alongside emotional images and videos, he called on Christians to fight against the "racism destroying generations," a racism that is, a photo he posted claimed, "so American, that when you protest against it, people think you are protesting America." If you take a look at his posts from this time, you'll recognize many familiar names of evangelical leaders who expressed support for his words. Even some conservative Christians echoed similar messages on Instagram. Dissent was rare because it was so vehemently opposed.

"Riots are the voice of the unheard" was the retort to concerns about the violence, looting, and arson done in the name of Floyd and the BLM movement. "No good cops in a racist system" was the response to the defense of police officers who do their job well. People who denied their own racism were accused of being fragile. People who questioned the existence or extent of systemic racism were accused of perpetuating it. Anything other than acknowledging the pervasiveness of white supremacy and its role in George Floyd's death, and donating time, money, and words to the cause of Black Lives Matter and all of its initiatives, was condemned as bigotry.

Eventually, government bodies, corporations, and schools would implement policies meant to fight systemic racism, and cities across the country would remove funding from their police departments. This was more than just rhetoric. Days, weeks, and months would be filled with aggressive, sometimes deadly, protests, with participants demanding the demolition of policing and revolutionary change to American systems.

The pressure was on to say the correct things on social media at the time. Everyone felt the need to prove that they were on the right side of history. It was more intense for Christians. If Christians believe all people are made in God's image, that we're to love our neighbor, and that racism is sin, shouldn't we be on board with Black Lives Matter? Shouldn't we want to abolish white supremacy and systemic injustice? Are you really a Christian if you oppose these things? Aren't Christians called to empathy?

So, that morning, I wrestled with posting the black square, posting nothing at all, or expressing my concerns about the whole situation instead. I chose the last option.

A few days later, I shared a video of an older woman, who was black, expressing through sobs her experience of watching her community devastated by rioters. The point of my post was to ask: Why not both? Why can't we be upset by the footage of George Floyd and condemn the riots? If the goal is justice, the protection of life, shouldn't we care about both?

While many agreed, I was also met with an onslaught of angry comments arguing it's disrespectful and—yes—*racist* to compare destruction of property to the killing of a human being. Buildings have insurance, they said, but Floyd's life can't be rebuilt. "Have some empathy," they chided, over and over again.

But this was about more than insurance claims. That property was people's homes, their businesses, their ability to feed their family, where they buy medicine and access necessary services. Innocent people, many of whom looked like George Floyd, were being punished for the actions of a police officer they didn't know. "How is this justice?" I wondered.

In the ensuing months, at least twenty-five people would die due to violence between protesters and rioters, including several black Americans.[3] I continued to ask the same question: Why not both? Why should the death of George Floyd be deemed more worthy of our outrage than, say, the deaths of David Dorn, Antonio Mays, Jr., and eight-year-old Secoriea Turner—all black Americans killed by people rioting in the name of racial justice?

In the same post, I also questioned the conclusion that George Floyd's death was motivated by racism. How do we know? Instead of an answer, I was met with accusations of hate. Hate that I should replace, of course, with empathy.

Empathy, apparently, would bid me to agree with Black Lives Matter. Empathy would help me excuse rioting and violence in the name of racial justice. Empathy would confirm that George Floyd's death was indeed the result of white supremacy. Empathy would demand that I uproot the racist systems upon which our country and our police system were founded. Empathy would open my eyes to the fact that racism is all around us.

Then and now, in the world of social media activism, outrage is considered the measure of virtue, but only outrage going in the "right" direction. We must show empathy, but only the "right" kind of empathy. The overwhelmingly loud voices online, joined by most of the mainstream media, Silicon Valley, academia, our public education system, our federal bureaucracy, and Hollywood, have decided that the outrage and empathy must align with progressive causes. Thus, in the summer of 2020, the only acceptable approach was to claim that systemic racism, alive and well in America since 1619, murdered George Floyd. I'd expressed the wrong kind of outrage.

I was facing weaponized, toxic empathy, and I had a couple of choices: delete the post, apologize, and acquiesce to their points; or stand by my words.

In the months that followed the black square craze, I pored over studies and books on race, history, justice, and economics by conservative authors like Thomas Sowell and Walter Williams, as well as books on critical race theory written by its most prominent proponents. I listened to the perspectives of Christians and non-Christians across the political spectrum. I talked to dozens of people on all sides of the issue. And everything I learned increased my confidence that too many Christians had been erroneously manipulated by toxic empathy when it came to so-called racial and social justice. They weren't willing to hear competing data or arguments to their narrative, because to do so would seem unempathetic.

But their claims were hurting people. They were stoking undue resentment among black Christians and unjustified guilt among white Christians. They were confusing their congregants and followers on what biblical justice really looks like. And they were adding to the voices that convinced government officials to enact policies like reducing policing in certain areas, the consequence of which has only been more crime, chaos, and death.

That's the danger of being led by empathy rather than by truth-filled love. You latch on to what sounds and feels good rather than what *is* good, often to the detriment of the very people you think you're trying to help. And it impacts much more than debates about policing or racism.

Red Flags and Real Hope

Kindness is good, and empathy can be good too. But empathy that affirms sin or lies is always misguided. How can we tell when empathy has become toxic? How can we tell when the point of an emotionally charged argument isn't to help us love someone but instead to approve of a damaging progressive agenda?

Here are a few red flags that we'll see repeatedly in these pages:

1. THE USE OF EUPHEMISMS: Euphemisms obscure the truth to make a position seem more palatable. Think "reproductive rights" for killing an unborn child, or "gender-affirming care" for bodily mutilation. In every conversation, advertisement, article, or podcast, you must carefully look out for the use of euphemisms. Ask yourself, "What does she mean by that?" and try to identify the reality her language choice is hiding.

2. CONTRADICTIONS TO GOD'S WORD: Sometimes these contradictions are obvious (e.g., "Jesus isn't the only way to heaven"), but most of the time, they're not. Just like the Devil tricking Eve or tempting Jesus, unbiblical statements are often paired with something true. Think "Christians are called to love the foreigner" to justify chaotic border laws, or "The early church shared everything they had" to justify socialism. Just because something sounds good doesn't mean it is. It's crucial we know our Bible and train ourselves

to think critically about the things we read and hear—especially when they're viral or catchy.

3. EXCLUSIVELY POLITICAL ENDS: When calling for empathy, inclusivity, and love, are they talking about how we treat these people as individuals, or are they actually speaking of achieving certain political ends? For example, "love is love" isn't really a call for us to love gay people by recognizing their innate worth as human beings and treat them with kindness; it's a call to legally redefine marriage and family. "Black lives matter" isn't just a true statement about the value of black people; it's a call to political change, which typically includes removing funding from police forces and redistributing wealth to black Americans. These are examples of the exploitation of empathy to achieve political power, not peace.

4. CHRISTIAN-SOUNDING WORDS WITH UNCHRISTIAN MEANINGS: The concepts of equality, equity, liberation, oppression, inclusion, and social justice can all be, in some way, found in the Bible, but the Bible defines them differently than progressive activists do. Biblical equity, for example, means fair, impartial judgment (Ps. 99:4). Progressive equity means equal outcomes. As Vice President Kamala Harris explained, "Equitable treatment means we all end up in the same place."4 As we will discuss in the social justice chapter, equal outcomes are impossible outside of extreme, oppressive government intervention, and nowhere does the Bible indicate that justice means everyone having equal resources.

5. EMOTIONAL LANGUAGE: Manipulative rhetoric lacks substantive, logical arguments and replaces them with demands that you feel a certain way. If you're really loving, caring, understanding, empathetic, etc., you will buy into a particular position. Often,

your rational points will be rebuffed with accusations of callousness instead of thoughtful responses. When they call you hateful, bigoted, racist, or any other epithet, it usually means they don't know why they believe what they believe, so their insecurity manifests itself in anger. This kind of bullying is frustrating, but you have the power to let it roll off your shoulders. I've learned from experience that it's best never to lose your cool and never to give an ounce of legitimacy to their insults. If they raise a fair point, say so, but don't waste your time defending yourself against their accusations. No need to say something like, "I'm not a bigot, but . . ." This shows you've at least registered their name-calling. You know such an allegation is ridiculous, and you don't need to dignify it with a response. Simply continue to kindly, humbly, but confidently stand your ground. It may be that this conversation planted a seed in them that won't blossom until much later on.

When these red flags show up, it means someone is using toxic empathy to capitalize on the Christian's righteous desire to be compassionate to the outcast and the weak, distorting biblical love into progressive activism and manipulating women into supporting issues that are harmful and, in many cases, sinful.

In the coming chapters, we'll see just how toxic empathy is deployed—and how it can be overcome—on the biggest issues today: abortion, transgenderism, "gay marriage," illegal immigration, and social justice. On each of these subjects, the progressive left uses real-life tragedies and trendy slogans to manipulate well-meaning people like you and me.

For example, to promote infanticide, they tell us "abortion is health care." To destroy God-ordained sex differences, they say "trans women are women." To pressure us to accept "gay marriage," they declare "love is love." To promote open borders, they assert "no human is illegal." And to radically reshape an America they've deemed racist, sexist, transphobic, and more, they insist that "social justice is justice."

We'll start each chapter by introducing an emotional story meant to draw you to the progressive position on the issue. Then we'll look at opposing anecdotes and debunk the left-wing arguments using factual and biblical truth.

When you finish this book, I hope you'll not only be able to spot and counter toxic empathy; I pray that you'll have a deeper love for both God's Word and a greater understanding of the world around you. And ultimately, I hope you'll be better equipped to introduce those with whom you disagree to the freeing love of Jesus.

Toxic Empathy

"Abortion Is Health Care"

If I know anything at all about God . . .
I know that God hates abortion.[1]

—R. C. SPROUL

HALO CASIANO WAS BORN in an East Texas hospital on March 29, 2023, weighing just three pounds. She lived for only four hours, taking her last breath wrapped in the arms of her father, Luis.

Halo was born with an underdeveloped skull and brain, the result of a birth defect called anencephaly. Babies who suffer from anencephaly are often stillborn, or survive a few days, at most, after birth.

Samantha, Halo's mom, was devastated by the diagnosis she received at her twenty-week anatomy scan. This was the little girl she'd hoped for, wanted, and for nearly five months, loved. When her doctor informed her that the baby's defect made her incompatible with life, she knew she needed an abortion.

To her surprise, however, that option wasn't available. While she was aware that Texas had enacted further abortion restrictions since the overturning of *Roe v. Wade* in 2022, she thought that her daughter's diagnosis would create an exception. But Texas's laws only permit abortions when the mother's life is in danger, like when there is an ectopic pregnancy (where the baby is growing outside the uterus, usually in the fallopian tube).

She had no choice but to carry the pregnancy to term. The weeks leading up to delivery were hellish, sending Samantha into a state of deep depression. As much as she loved her daughter, she dreaded watching her suffer and die.

"I didn't want to go to the doctor's office," she told NPR, who first reported on her story. "I don't want to sound hateful, but I don't want to see all these pregnant women, and I'm over here carrying a baby—I love my baby, but she should be at rest by now. I just keep thinking that over and over again—my baby should be at rest, I shouldn't have to put her through this."

Samantha quickly learned that simultaneously preparing for your baby's birth and death is not only traumatic, it's expensive. Living in a mobile home with four of her own children—including her nine-month-old daughter—as well as her goddaughter, she and Luis didn't have funds to spare for a funeral, for which she was quoted a price of four thousand dollars.

At thirty-three weeks gestation, still unsure how they'd overcome these seemingly insurmountable challenges, Samantha endured a painful delivery and finally met her wanted, fragile baby girl, Halo. She spent her last moments in the presence of parents who loved her and would have done anything to make her whole.

Managing to put together the funds to provide a funeral for Halo, Samantha and Luis buried their daughter on Good Friday.

Samantha vowed never to get pregnant again.

What "Empathy" Demands

Samantha's story is heartbreaking. As a mom, I can feel the pain she must have suffered during and after pregnancy. Imagining those precious, gut-wrenching hours after Halo's birth—holding her, tracing her little face, feeling her tiny grip on your finger, hoping against hope that maybe the doctors were wrong.

Maybe she's the exception, you think. Maybe she's the girl who'll defy all odds and live, fulfilling all the dreams you had for her. Then collapsing with an excruciating, confusing mixture of sadness and relief as you realize she's breathed her last breath, and that the daughter you'd carried and cared for would never grow up. You'd never hear her laugh, see her walk, know her personality. She's gone, and now you have to go home without her, facing the cold reality of everyday life's relentless demands. There's nothing that could prepare you for that.

I've now birthed three children. Like all moms, I remember everything: the surprise and excitement of the first positive pregnancy test, the first kicks, the nerves before the twenty-week scan, the anticipation and misery of the last few weeks of pregnancy, and the endless layers of emotional and physical experiences that accompany labor and delivery.

The love that you have for these children you've grown and birthed is indescribable and consuming. I'm sure Samantha felt what I feel as a mother—that I would do absolutely anything, make any sacrifice, for my children. I'd take their pain, if I could, do anything to ensure their well-being. Having children truly is like having your heart walk around outside your body. There's nothing simultaneously more painful and joy-inducing.

I first read Samantha's story in a piece by NPR, published a few weeks after Halo's birth. The article and accompanying Instagram post were clearly written to evoke sadness and anger, specifically from women like me, regarding the injustice of the family's situation. The comments underneath the article and post echo the piece's intent: That she was forced to carry the pregnancy post-diagnosis, forced to give birth, and forced to pay for a funeral, we read, is the unfair and cruel consequence of abortion restrictions and the overturning of *Roe*.

NPR seeks to solicit empathy toward Samantha, asking readers to put themselves in her shoes. The implicit questions are obvious: How awful would it be to carry a pregnancy you knew would end in the death of your baby? How stressful would it be to plan a funeral for your child while working, trying to make ends meet, and taking care of both yourself and your baby? How much easier would it have been for Samantha if she'd been able to have an abortion at twenty weeks? What if this were you? Would you want to endure this kind of painful ordeal? Shouldn't we remove abortion restrictions so tragic stories like Samantha's won't happen again? Plus, isn't abortion just "reproductive health"—another part of women's health care?

There was a time when I would have been the target audience for a story like Samantha's.

When I was growing up, topics like abortion were rarely discussed. I lived in the "before time"—pre the craziness of social media and nonstop news. My friends and I felt no pressure to have a formulated position on every social issue of the day. At the time, I didn't even really know what the abortion procedure entailed. I was just intuitively pro-life. Before my belief that killing a baby in the womb was wrong was the conviction that premarital sex should be avoided, both to align with biblical purity and to exclude the possibility of an unwanted pregnancy. Abortion was simply one component in the network of sexual no-nos that occupied my brain as a kid raised in a Christian home.

But while I called myself pro-life through and after college, I held on to the belief that there were exceptions depending on the circumstances of the pregnancy. As a woman, I could have imagined myself in a woman like Samantha's position. I would have felt empathy for someone forced to endure such a trying few months. I would have agreed with NPR's implication—that these pro-life laws had gone too far and lacked compassion for dire situations like this one.

But today, even as a mother who can now more acutely understand the pain Samantha must have felt, I don't draw the same conclusion. My mind changed several years ago when, in response to a Facebook post I made stating what I thought was my staunchly pro-life position that abortion should be illegal except in cases of rape, incest, fetal abnormalities, and perhaps some other cases, someone challenged me. They asked a simple question: What's the difference between a child conceived in rape and a child not conceived in rape? In other words, why are diagnoses or the circumstances surrounding a person's conception justification for killing them?

I'd never thought about it in that way, because I wasn't considering abortion from the perspective of the child the procedure kills. I had fallen victim to toxic empathy, manipulated into thinking of only one part of the story without realizing what I was missing.

The fact is, abortion purposely kills an innocent person. In Samantha's story, that would have been Halo.

Where is the compassion—the empathy—for her? She was a living human being. Did her diagnosis justify an abortion?

Let's look at Samantha and Halo's story another way.

The Flip Side of Empathy

As always, there's a flip side to the one-sided empathy narrative.

As Christians, as thinkers, and as truth-seekers—people who care about what is "good, right, and true" (Eph. 5:9) as well as what's loving—we're required to go beyond putting ourselves in Samantha's shoes. We must consider this story from Halo's perspective.

An uncomfortable, often ignored truth is that, whether via abortion or birth, a baby is still delivered. If Samantha had been able to access an abortion at twenty weeks, she would have had to endure an extremely involved, painful procedure to end Halo's life—and she would still have had to deliver her child.

At twenty weeks gestation, the baby would have been small (about the size of a banana) but fully formed. She would have been aborted using one of two methods: an aspiration abortion or a dilation and extraction (D&X) procedure.

An aspiration abortion, which is typically performed between ten- and sixteen-weeks gestation, would have removed the baby via suction. First, the abortion provider places sticks called laminaria into the woman's cervix twenty-four to forty-eight hours before her procedure. This both opens the cervix and soaks up the amniotic fluid in the uterus, which is necessary for the baby's survival. Because of this, the baby is sometimes already dead by the time of the actual procedure, but many times they are not. Dead or alive, during the abortion, the baby's limbs, torso, and skull are sucked out of the uterus using a vacuum tube.

In a D&X abortion, which is usually reserved for babies after sixteen weeks of pregnancy, the abortion procedure starts the same way an aspiration abortion does—with laminaria to dilate the cervix. But because the baby is too big to be sucked out with a vacuum tube, her actual killing and removal requires more steps.

To "ensure fetal demise," as the abortion industry describes it, the baby is killed by the abortionist inserting a needle filled with digoxin or potassium chloride—the same poisonous chemical combination used in lethal injection for convicted murderers on death row—through the mother's abdomen into the uterus and the amniotic sac, and, if the baby stops wiggling long enough, the abortionist injects the poison directly into her heart.

When the poison is released into the amniotic sac, the baby consumes it and dies. When the poison is injected through her chest and into her heart, she has a heart attack that kills her.

At this point in the pregnancy, the baby is so big, and her movements have become so strong, that without the numbing medication that is used for women during this procedure, the mother would be able to feel her punch and kick as she dies. The baby is developed enough to see, hear, and, depending on her age, feel the pain of the abortion. While the existence of flinching, crying, and screaming by the child being aborted has been debated by doctors, I don't think we will ever know the horrific sights and sounds in the womb during an abortion. I think we'd go mad if we did.

And even more horrifically, abortions don't always "succeed" in killing the baby.

In 2013, registered nurse Jill Stanek testified before the House Judiciary Committee about her time working in the Labor and Delivery ward of Christ Hospital in Oak Lawn, Illinois. She described what it was like to discover that babies who survived abortions were being placed in a utility closet to die. She said: "I was traumatized and changed forever by my experience of holding a little abortion survivor for forty-five minutes until he died, a twenty-one or twenty-two-week-old baby who had been aborted because he had Down Syndrome."[2]

Because there are only six states that require reporting of children who survive abortions, stories like Stanek's are more likely than we know. The Center for Disease Control and Prevention (CDC) estimates that between 2003 and 2014, there were at least 143 babies who died after being born alive after an abortion procedure.[3] There is a significant probability that that number is much higher.

In 2005, a mother attempted to undergo an abortion at twenty-three-weeks gestation at EPOC Clinic in Orlando, Florida, only to deliver her living, moving son in a toilet. She begged the staff to help, and they not only refused but turned away paramedics. She cradled her son and sang to him for eleven minutes until he died.[4]

Sycloria Williams sought an abortion in 2006. She delivered her twenty-three-week baby at A Gyn Diagnostic Center in Hialeah, Florida. When she began breathing and moving, the owner of the clinic reportedly quickly cut the umbilical cord and left the child to suffocate in a sealed biohazard bag.[5]

Infamously, now imprisoned abortionist Kermit Gosnell admitted to delivering babies and snipping their spinal cords as they were exiting the birth canal.[6] It's difficult to imagine a more gut-wrenching scene: the life of a fully formed, viable child, on the verge of her first breath, preparing to instinctively search for her mother, violently snuffed out.

Late-term-abortion provider LeRoy Carhart, who died in 2023, explained in a 1997 court testimony how he performs third-trimester abortions: by injecting the poison digoxin into the baby's heart and inducing labor a few days later, so that by the time the dead, limp baby exits the mother's womb, the baby's body is like, as he said later, "meat in a crock-pot."[7] In his testimony, he admitted that the baby wasn't always dead when he induced the abortion. In that case, he would have had to crush the living baby's skull and dismember her to ensure her demise.

While abortions at or after twenty-one weeks gestation are rarer than abortions earlier in the second trimester and in the third trimester, they still happen. The CDC puts the number at about ten thousand per year.[8] However, the number is likely far higher, as only a handful of states are required to report their numbers on late-term abortions.

You might be wondering "What about earlier abortions, then? Aren't those better?"

It's true that most abortions happen in the first trimester. But scientifically, these babies are still equally human. They're just smaller and less developed. And killing them is still brutal.

Through twelve weeks gestation, women typically undergo medication abortions. First, the mother is given a pill called mifepristone. Mifepristone blocks the hormone progesterone, which is necessary for the new life to grow. Without progesterone, the lining of the uterus breaks down, which makes it impossible for the embryo or fetus to continue to grow. Essentially, the baby is starved of nutrients and dies. The second step is to give the mother misoprostol, which causes the uterus to contract and expel her baby. After a few hours of heavy cramping and bleeding, a "successful" first trimester abortion is complete—often at home, without a doctor's supervision.

As a reminder, a baby's heart starts beating at about six weeks gestation. That's only two weeks after a missed period. Despite desperate attempts by the media to belittle these heartbeats as "pulses," doctors have long acknowledged this cardiac activity is, indeed, a heartbeat, even if the heart is still developing.[9]

Abortion isn't health care. What other form of health care involves killing a human being? Abortion is a vicious practice, no matter when it happens and no matter how much empathy we have for mothers in tough situations.

Yet there are still many understandable questions about the what-ifs of abortion and pregnancy emergencies. What if, for example, the mother's life is at risk?

The pro-life position was articulated well by obstetrician-gynecologist Dr. Monique Chireau Wubbenhorst, who explained in a 2023 hearing before a Senate Judiciary Committee hearing on abortion law: "When you're performing a procedure to save the life of the mother, it is not morally considered an abortion. Therefore, it is ethically permissible. . . . You act in the best interest of both patients. If the death of the unborn child is a result of your intervention, that is a tragic outcome, but nonetheless, our priority is to save the life of the mother. . . . That can be accomplished without performing an abortion."[10]

In other words, in a situation where the mother's physical life is at risk, the baby should be delivered, and, if medically possible, helped to survive. In some cases, like when the complication occurs early in the pregnancy, the baby's survival isn't possible, so the mom must be saved by delivering her child. This is very different, scientifically and morally, from purposely and violently killing the baby inside the womb.

In Halo's case, Samantha would still have delivered had she chosen abortion, but rather than delivering an intact baby she would have instead delivered a child mangled by forceps whom she and Luis would have never been able to hold, see, kiss, or tell "I love you." Halo would have been unceremoniously discarded by hospital staff and waste management rather than buried in the presence of her family.

Is that truly the loving option? Is that really the outcome that justice demands?

Of course not.

Both Samantha and Halo deserved compassion and love, not faux empathy that would have ended in the purposeful, violent ending of a baby's life. Toxic empathy urges us to focus on only one part of Samantha's story. True love demands that we look at the fullness of both Samantha's and Halo's lives.

The Key to the Abortion Debate

While Samantha's pregnancy was painful, and while the delivery, Halo's subsequent death, and the costly funeral all make for an unimaginably tragic circumstance, the trauma endured by Samantha doesn't outweigh the reality of abortion: it takes a human life.

Halo was a human being from the moment of conception. She was alive. She had a sex that was determined when sperm met egg. In fact, *all* of her DNA was determined at fertilization. She wasn't a tissue, a tumor, an organ, or a lifeless clump of cells. She was a unique human who was, as all of us were at our beginning stages, developing. This isn't scientifically debatable.

The disagreement is really centered on whether that little human is a *person*—with value and rights. There has been much debate around what makes a human a person. Is it sentience? Age? Independence?

Princeton philosopher Peter Singer, for example, infamously supports the idea that babies, while scientifically human, are not human persons. His reasoning goes like this:

1. We must treat all persons according to moral guidelines.

2. Persons are self-aware.

3. Infants are not self-aware and thus are not persons. We do not need to treat them according to moral guidelines.

Logically, then, that means that babies under a year and a half don't have rights, including the right to life. Thus, if parents decide they want to kill their baby, according to Singer's logic, they can.

Most people who consider themselves "pro-choice" would find Singer's argument abominable. They're empathetic, after all, and empathetic people don't support murdering toddlers.

But what they don't realize is that *everyone* who advocates for abortion, in any trimester, has adopted a logic identical to Singer's.

If we acknowledge that a baby in the womb (or fetus, embryo, or zygote—it doesn't matter, because they're all different stages of human development, like infancy and adulthood) is indeed a human being, then there needs to be some kind of reasonable justification on the part of abortion advocates for purposely ending their life.

Why are these the human beings that the law should allow us to murder, while we don't support legal murder for anyone outside the womb?

Is it because she's small?

Is it that he's inside his mother's womb?

Is it that her attachment to her mother keeps her alive?

Is it that he's at the earliest stages of his life?

Is it that she lacks self-awareness?

Is it because he's unwanted, poor, or diagnosed with a disability?

Is it because she was conceived in a horrific case of rape or incest?

Why are these reasonable justifications for killing a human in the womb, but not outside the womb?

In what other situations should we use size, location, dependence, age, sentience, poverty, disability, abuse, or conception circumstances to advocate for the extermination of people who have already been born?

Those who advocate for the legality of abortion make the separation between born humans and preborn humans because we've all been fed a steady diet of lies—from the media, from Hollywood, from the multibillion-dollar abortion industry, and from the government—that abortion is a different, more acceptable form of murder. Actually, we're told it's not murder at all. It's "planning parenthood." It's "reproductive freedom." It's "bodily autonomy." It's "women's rights." It's not a baby that's being killed, it's "pregnancy termination," the removal of a "clump of cells."

People on the side of abortion use all kinds of euphemisms, half-truths, and straight-up lies to obscure what the procedure is and does. "Baby murder" simply isn't good PR, so sterilized, misleading, unscientific terminology is adopted to make what's always the gruesome killing of an innocent human more palatable to the public.

A good rule of thumb is this: if you're on the right side of an issue, you don't have to lie to convince people to join you.

The truth is, every person who considers themselves "pro-choice," no matter what they *say* they believe, has accepted Peter Singer's reasoning that human value and rights start sometime after birth. The core of this logic is that personhood is granted to others by those who have the power to do so. This is the truth masked by fake, empathy-based narratives about abortion.

If we define personhood as anything *other* than being human, which happens at the moment of fertilization, we're in arbitrary, dangerous territory—dangerous territory that Western societies have traveled into before.

The Dark History of Abortion

The sixth of eleven surviving children, Margaret Higgins Sanger saw early on the burden children and childbearing placed on women. Sanger's mother endured multiple miscarriages, which weakened her body, and she died from tuberculosis at age fifty.

Sanger saw a dire need to prevent pregnancies—not just for women's well-being but also for the sake of eliminating poverty and hereditary disease. Ultimately, she wanted a "clean" race of humanity that wouldn't weigh the world down with its neediness, which meant popularizing contraception and discouraging the fertility of women— usually poor working-class and black people—whose large families, she believed, were holding them back.

Early in her activism career, Sanger was indicted for writing and disseminating literature about the importance of contraception—what she nicknamed "birth control"—and instead of standing trial, she fled

America for Britain. While there, she refined her justifications for her antireproduction campaign through interactions with the Malthusian League.

In many ways, Thomas Malthus—the namesake of the Malthusian League—was Sanger's intellectual predecessor. Malthus warned that overpopulation would lead to the dwindling of resources, which would lead to a deadly decline in living standards. The proposed solution to his Malthusian catastrophe was to limit the growth of the population as much as possible.

Malthus's theory, however, was wrong. While the world population has increased by seven billion people since 1800,[11] extreme poverty has decreased from 84 percent to 24 percent.[12] As it turns out, human beings *add* to and benefit our environments more than we subtract and detract from them.

However, in the nineteenth and twentieth centuries, many thinkers shared Malthus's concerns about the impending doom wrought by the existence of too many people. This gave rise to advocacy for eugenics. English naturalist Sir Francis Galton, the half-cousin of Charles Darwin, birthed the field of eugenics in 1883, which he defined as "the science which deals with all influences that improve the inborn qualities of a race."[13] A common idea among supporters of eugenics was that certain ethnicities were innately inferior, both intellectually and morally.

Galton argued that social ills such as poverty and crime were driven largely by unfavorable hereditary characteristics. Some ethnicities, he believed, were innately inferior, both intellectually and morally, and thus he rejected the "unreasonable" sentiment "against the gradual extinction of an inferior race."[14]

His ideas gained steam, most famously in Germany. Beginning in 1933, the Nazi government mandated the forced sterilization of those with disabilities, legalized abortion for non-Germans and the mentally ill, and criminalized marriage or sexual relations between Jews and non-Jewish Germans. The culmination of Germany's agenda of *rassenhygiene*, or racial purity, was the Holocaust: the extermination of six million Jewish people, whom Hitler and the Nazi Party blamed for the deterioration of German society, as well as millions of others deemed impure or unfit to live.

This is the philosophical legacy of Planned Parenthood and Margaret Sanger, who forged a plot in the United States to minimize—if not eradicate—the existence of people she considered undesirable. Her plans quickly bore fruit.

In 1927, the Supreme Court ruling in *Buck v. Bell* effectively agreed, ruling mass sterilization was constitutional. Justice Oliver Wendell Holmes Jr. declared: "Three generations of imbeciles are enough."[15]

Sanger was especially concerned about limiting black births, writing to the heir of the Procter & Gamble fortune that "the most successful educational approach to the Negro is through a religious appeal. We don't want the word to get out that we want to exterminate the Negro population, and the minister is the man who can straighten out that idea if it ever occurs to any of their more rebellious members."[16]

But the horrors of the Holocaust and the worldwide sympathy it evoked eventually forced Sanger and her eugenicist contemporaries to update their message. In 1942, the American Birth Control League dropped "birth control" from their messaging and used the term "planned parenthood" instead.[17] The new organization, Planned Parenthood, would shift its focus from breeding a pure racial stock to encouraging the use of contraception, offering abortions, and providing infertility treatments.

Yet the eugenicist legacy persisted. Planned Parenthood's president in 1973—when *Roe v. Wade* was decided by the U.S. Supreme Court—was Dr. Alan F. Guttmacher, former vice president of the

American Eugenics Society. Today his name adorns the Guttmacher Institute, the premier research organization of the abortion industry.

Despite dropping "population control" and "eugenics" from its public list of goals, Planned Parenthood has followed the eugenics program to its inevitable conclusion. Of the hundreds of thousands of abortions performed each year in the United States, 39.2 percent are undergone by black women, despite this demographic making up only about 12.4 percent of the U.S. population as of 2020.[18] In 2013, more black babies in New York City were aborted than born.[19] These statistics alone satisfy Sanger's founding vision for her movement.

The partnership between eugenics, depopulation, and abortion is still prominent. Microsoft cofounder and activist Bill Gates is a major investor in providing worldwide access to birth control for the purpose of curbing population growth. In a 2010 TED Talk, he warned: "The world today has 6.8 billion people. That's headed up to about 9 billion. . . . Now, if we do a really great job on new vaccines, health care, reproductive health services, we could lower that by, perhaps, ten or fifteen percent."[20]

Billionaire Warren Buffett, the sixth richest man on earth, has given more than $1 billion in grants to pro-abortion organizations like Planned Parenthood, the Guttmacher Institute, and the National Abortion Federation, driven by what biographer Roger Lowenstein called "a Malthusian dread" of overpopulation. Buffett is also one of the original investors in RU-486 (a U.S. abortion pill) manufacturer Danco Laboratories.[21]

Charlie Munger, who was the vice chairman of Buffett's investing firm, Berkshire Hathaway, until his death in 2023, worked with Buffett to found a "church" in the 1960s that wasn't really a religious entity but rather existed to aid women in obtaining abortions outside the United States.[22]

The Rockefellers, another billionaire family, have supported abortion efforts for decades. According to the Rockefeller Brothers Fund, John D. Rockefeller Jr. had a focus on "special projects in African-American communities."[23]

Gates, Buffett, and the Rockefellers are only a portion of the Malthus-motivated American elites funding abortion. With unquantifiable power and prestige, the world's billionaires carry the torch of the population control industry's doctrine of death.

Abortion supporters may feel genuine empathy for those on the margins and believe they are providing ways to alleviate pain. Maybe Sanger felt the same way. But that empathy is inextricably intertwined with evil ideas like eugenics and population control.

There is no compassion, no love, no humanity, no goodness to abortion.

Not ever, and not today.

The "Holistically Pro-Life" Lie

Abortion advocates typically accuse those who are pro-life of lacking empathy for mothers. We're told that pro-lifers only care about the unborn child and do nothing to support their mothers, who often become pregnant under difficult circumstances.

Christians are especially vulnerable to this argument. The desire to care for not just preborn babies, but their mothers, fathers, and communities, too, is not only admirable, but necessary. These individuals and groups are correct in asserting that the biblical position is one of compassion toward all kinds of people, including the preborn baby, the unwed mother, the refugee, and those who are in poverty.

There are many Christians who consider themselves "holistically pro-life," "pro–all life," or supporters of people from "womb to tomb." While they would say abortion is important, there are other issues that also fall under the "pro-life" umbrella and in fact may impact how many women seek abortions each year. Often, but not always, this category of Christians disagrees with legal bans on abortion and insists on rectifying other social ills rather than limiting abortion access.

In a now deleted video posted to his YouTube channel in 2020, Christian musician Lecrae articulated this exact idea: "You're saying, 'Hey, don't terminate the life of the child.' Well, you've got to remember that there's all these different issues coming into play for certain individuals that no one is addressing. . . . If you just outlaw something, I know for a fact that's not going to be the solution."

While he does say that outlawing may still be a valid option, his argument minimizes the importance of the legal fight against abortion, deeming it ultimately ineffective, in favor of addressing other issues he believes will create a more holistic culture of life.

Christian author and podcaster Jamie Ivey has advanced a similar view. In a podcast interview, Ivey pushed back against what she sees as the "traditional pro-life perspective," which is to advocate exclusively for the preborn. She encourages "white Evangelicals" to broaden their compassion to include "other injustices in other human dignity spaces," like immigration, and asserts that it is equally important to advocate for the mother's well-being as it is to fight for the life of her child.

In sum, many of these "pro–all life" arguments suggest that compassion demands we give less of our attention to preventing abortion and more attention to improving the lives of women and to causes other than abortion. Advocates of this position are typically hesitant to support legal restrictions on abortions.

However subtle, this is toxic empathy in action. It takes attention away from the true victim of abortion—the baby—and her legal right to life, and instead focuses only on the pregnant woman.

The truth is, the pro-life movement is already going above and beyond to meet the needs of women. They're just not waiting for the government to do the job they know God has called them to do themselves. In addition to advocating for laws that protect the lives of babies, pro-lifers are serving women and families in incredible, transformational ways.

Truth and Love in Action

Every day, thousands of pregnant women are shown true care by pregnancy centers. According to *The New York Times*, pregnancy centers are "largely run by conservative Christians,"[24] a fact that anyone who has entered a pregnancy center can tell you. These facilities service thousands of mothers and babies every year by providing them with free pregnancy tests, ultrasounds, prenatal vitamins, parenting classes, education courses, adoption information, pregnancy and baby items—and most important, genuine love. As of 2021, there were about three thousand of these centers in the United States, and data from 2019 shows that they have served over two million people.[25]

I've visited several centers across the country in both liberal and conservative states. I could fill pages with stories of abused, poor, young, scared, lonely, and rejected women whose needs were met for the very first time by the folks at pro-life pregnancy centers. But there is one story that brings me to tears every time I tell it.

I first came across the story of a refugee named Maria* in March 2023, when I interviewed Leanne Jamieson, director of Prestonwood Pregnancy Center in Dallas. Jamieson told me that days before she first met Maria, Maria went to Planned Parenthood seeking an abortion. She was unexpectedly pregnant, and with the father no longer in the

* Not her real name.

picture, she wanted an abortion. But when the Planned Parenthood employee informed Maria the procedure would cost hundreds of dollars, she was at a loss. She'd never be able to afford it.

So, she searched for other clinics in the area that might be able to help her for free. The first name to pop up on Google was Prestonwood Pregnancy Center. When she arrived there, she was greeted warmly. She met with a counselor who told her about her options, which included abortion, though they made clear they did not perform or refer for the procedure. She learned what the procedure entailed—something she didn't know and hadn't learned at Planned Parenthood. But most of the meeting was filled with the counselor's questions: What had brought her here? What was her living situation? Did she have a relationship with the baby's father? Does she attend church? What does she need that the center could provide for her?

She was taken aback by what seemed like sincere care and curiosity. Why did she matter to these strangers? What was she to them? How did they provide all of these services without charging her?

The counselor assured her they could help. They gave her prenatal vitamins and helped her with Medicaid enrollment. They signed her up for parenting classes. Just knowing there were people who cared assuaged her fears. They made her feel seen. They told her God loves her and sees her too. She hadn't heard that before. She decided to keep her baby.

When Maria began having painful contractions, she rushed to the hospital alone. Her first thought was to call the women at the pregnancy center to support her during labor, and Leanne met her at the hospital right away. When doctors determined that Maria was in false labor, she was sent home. As Leanne left the hospital, a nurse told her to make sure Maria has a car seat when she comes back.

It occurred to Leanne to check up on Maria at her home. While she keeps a relationship with her clients, usually they have someone else to call during labor. She had a feeling Maria did not have any support.

On her way to Maria's, she stopped by the pregnancy center and picked up a car seat from the stash of donated new car seats they kept in their storage closet. When Maria opened the door and saw Leanne, car seat in hand, she fell to her knees and broke into tears. Leanne didn't understand. She knelt down and asked, "Sweet one, what's wrong?"

"The nurse said . . . 'Listen, when you come back and you're in real labor, you need to have a car seat with you or you can't take your baby home.'"

Leanne's heart broke. She got up and stepped into Maria's apartment. As she looked around, she saw how little Maria had. The room was nearly bare, and the refrigerator and pantry were close to empty. There was no crib or other baby supplies.

Leanne told Maria, "Some of my friends are going to show up, and they're going to bring you some things that you need. Just let them in if they say they're a friend of mine." When Leanne got in the car, she made the necessary phone calls and soon went to Costco to get some supplies. When she returned to Maria's later that evening, she was moved by what she saw.

Maria opened the door crying and Leanne could hear voices in her bedroom. She walked in and some of the friends she had called were there constructing a crib and putting together the baby's nursery.

Leanne went back into the living room, where Maria was standing overwhelmed in tears. "Leanne, I thought God had forsaken me?" she said. "I thought he had turned his back on me."

Leanne answered, "Sweet one, God has heard your cry." Leanne shared the gospel with Maria, which, by now, Maria had heard from her and others at Prestonwood Pregnancy Center several times. But this time, watching this good news tangibly play out in front of her, seeing this love in action, it clicked.

The next week, Maria was baptized. Days later, she gave birth to a healthy baby girl, Leanne by her side.

Months later, Maria and her daughter participated in a baby dedication ceremony at Prestonwood. When the pastor introduced them, he shared a bit of their story—how Maria had chosen life for her baby with the help of the volunteers at the pregnancy center. When he'd finished the introduction, the entire congregation erupted into applause, which grew into a roaring standing ovation. Maria looked into the faces of thousands of her fellow church members and wept with joy.

This story isn't an anomaly. This is what pro-life Christians do. They show up, in big and small ways. They meet needs. They love— before, during, and after birth. "We need to do more for women" is not an excuse to support the legal killing of children. It's toxic empathy masking the brutality of abortion and obscuring the reality that the work is *already* being done. The only question is whether we will choose to be a part of it.

Anti–Pregnancy Center Propaganda

Of course, the pro-abortion side doesn't want you to know this about pro-lifers and the centers they run. They are incentivized both by profit and ideology to villainize the people keeping pregnant women out of abortion clinics.

As pro-life advocate and former Planned Parenthood employee Abby Johnson has recounted on my podcast, *Relatable*: "If a woman decides to parent her child, that's where our assistance stops at Planned Parenthood because we don't provide any prenatal care. We don't have any resources for her: baby items, diapers, anything like that. So essentially, she becomes a person who is not revenue-generating for us. We don't want her in our doors anymore. . . . She's now become a money drain on us, a time-suck on us, so we send her out the door. The only way that we could keep our patients as revenue-generating clients was to sell them an abortion." To do that, Abby told me, women are persuaded to believe abortion is a regret-free, uncomplicated, standard health-care option while they are routinely lied to about gestation, fetal development, and the risks.

It is no surprise that abortion advocates do everything in their power to inhibit the work of pregnancy centers, which provide actual choices for mothers. Here are some examples:

In June 2022, Democratic senator Elizabeth Warren was one of a group of Democratic senators to introduce a bill to "stop anti-abortion disinformation by crisis pregnancy centers," called the Stop Anti-Abortion Disinformation Act. Pregnancy centers could be fined $100,000 or 50 percent of their revenue for violating the act's "prohibition on disinformation," a term that would be defined by the Federal Trade Commission.[26]

In 2015, California lawmakers passed a bill forcing pregnancy centers to advertise state-provided abortions to their clientele. In 2018, the Supreme Court justly struck down the law as a violation of the right to free speech.[27]

Heidi Matzke, the president of Alternatives Pregnancy Center in California, testified to the Senate Judiciary Committee that a raging, machete-wielding man threatened her clinic.[28] A pregnancy center in Oregon was partly incinerated, apparently by pro-abortion terrorists, in June 2022.[29]

In April 2023, pro-abortion terrorist group Jane's Revenge defaced a pro-life center in Ohio.[30] Jane's Revenge has taken responsibility for a multitude of attacks on pregnancy centers across the country, often leaving behind their tagline: "If abortion isn't safe, neither are you."[31]

After the *Dobbs* decision was leaked in May 2022, authorities arrested Nicholas John Roske in the middle of an assassination attempt against Supreme Court Justice Brett Kavanaugh.[32]

It shouldn't surprise us that those who advocate for the legal dismemberment of innocent children are also violent in general. Of course, not all abortion advocates are terrorists. But because murder is the foundation of the movement, it's expected that its loudest, strongest activists will seek to inflict their enemies with pain and death.

The movement that labels itself pro-choice actually only pushes one outcome: abortion. In fact, it actively suppresses alternatives to abortion, shielding mothers from the realities of the procedure. Anyone who seeks an abortion at Planned Parenthood will be lied to about fetal development and will likely be prevented from seeing her ultrasound image.

Abortion providers use *empathy*—"I can imagine your situation, and a baby would be too hard to raise right now"—to lure women into believing abortion is their best option. Pregnancy centers like Prestonwood offer love and real support. As Christians, we have the option to be on the side of death and destruction and fake empathy, or we can be on the side of truth and love.

There's No Biblical Case for Abortion

There is no scientific, philosophical, moral, logical, or constitutional justification for abortion. But, most importantly, there's no biblical one either.

It's wrong to kill someone because, no matter what abortion advocates say, people *aren't* just clumps of cells. We're made in the image of God, which elevates us above the status of plants and animals

(Gen. 1:27). Humans, and humans alone, have souls. According to the creation account in Genesis, we matter more than any other part of creation. It was only after the creation of man and woman that God beheld the world and declared it not just good, but "very good" (Gen. 1:31).

While from the beginning of Scripture God allows, and even calls for, the killing of animals for food and for sacrifices, He expresses deep detestation for the unjust killing of people. In Genesis 4, God curses Cain for murdering his brother, Abel. In Genesis 9:6, in His covenant to Noah, God demands that the death penalty be carried out for murderers. He roots his reasoning for this punishment in a reality that is just as true today as it was then—human beings are valuable because man is made in His image.

While some killing in Scripture is clearly justified—just war and the death penalty for certain crimes, for example (more on that later)—murder, which is the killing of a legally innocent person, is not. The prohibition of murder is the fifth of the Ten Commandments given to Israel and is doubled down upon by Jesus (Ex. 20:13, Matt. 5:21–22). It is covered under the second greatest demand for Christians, which is to love our neighbor as ourselves (Rom. 13:9). Abortion is hateful, not loving.

Proverbs 6:16–17 lists "six things that the Lord hates," including "hands that shed innocent blood."

There are many professing Christians who try to justify abortion, or at least defend its legality, by misusing the Bible. Some may point to a strange passage in Numbers 5:11–31, which describes what's referred to as a "jealousy offering." If a man suspected that a wife had committed adultery, she would be made to imbibe a concoction, the physical effects of which would apparently show whether she had engaged in infidelity or not. There are many aspects of this seemingly bizarre ritual that we could debate and discuss, but the relevant point is that there is no evidence whatsoever that this passage describes or calls for an abortion.

Abortion defenders may also use the flood, the plagues, and the wars that God ordains to show that God himself doesn't regard life as sacred and therefore he would consider abortion permissible. I relate to this kind of confusion about God's character. I won't pretend to have perfectly packaged answers on every question that exists about the Bible or the nature of God. But my inability to understand the plans God carries out for his own glory doesn't obscure his clear commands.

If we love God, we will love the things he loves and hate the things he hates. If we love God, we will seek every means possible to protect voiceless, vulnerable children from the horror of abortion.

Christians have no reason to waver on, belittle, or push the abortion crisis to the side. We can and should care about all different kinds of people, both in and outside the womb, and the struggles they face. But all of this is a distraction from the central problem with abortion: it kills an innocent human being.

And if abortion kills an innocent human being—an image bearer of God—fighting to secure that baby's right to live is the first and most urgent order of business.

An End to Legal Abortion

It's very simple: laws restricting abortion save lives. In the six months following the overturning of *Roe v. Wade* in June 2022, there were thirty-two thousand fewer abortions nationwide than in the six months prior, due to the laws restricting abortions in Republican-run states.[33]

There's a chart that goes around each election cycle showing that the abortion rate is lower when a Democrat is president versus when a Republican is president. Pro-choicers say that Democrats, by providing more taxpayer-funded social services, make women less likely to choose abortion. But this is a classic correlation-causation fallacy. Democrat presidents don't cause the lower abortion rate and Republican presidents don't cause a higher rate, because presidents don't make abortion policy. Actually, the federal government rarely has a hand at all in passing laws that would affect abortion in any way. Most of these laws are passed at the state level. And considering, for example, that an unprecedented number of state legislatures were Republican-led while Obama was president, it's much more likely that state pro-life laws led to the decline of abortions during his tenure, not anything he signed with his pen.

According to Dr. Michael New, a researcher at the Charlotte Lozier Institute, Poland is the only developed country with nationwide protections for unborn babies. New asserts: "Since the early 1990s [when restrictions on abortion were instituted], the abortion rate in Poland has fallen by 76 percent. Similarly, the percentage of unintended pregnancies that are aborted fell from approximately 64 percent to 37 percent."[34]

These numbers represent real babies saved from the cold grip of forceps, from the pain of forced cardiac arrest, from the cruelty of poisoning. They symbolize real people who were given the chance to be born, to grow up, and to develop into people whose contributions we'll never be able to adequately measure.

These are people saved because the government, which God instituted to be his servant to do good and punish wrong (Rom. 13:4), recognized that they have the right to life and thus deemed their murder illegal.

And while it's true, as Lecrae pointed out, that some abortions will occur regardless of the law, that's true of all crimes. Just because theft and murder still happen despite the laws prohibiting them doesn't mean they should be made legal. When wrongdoing is legalized, more wrongdoing happens.

That's precisely what happened with abortion. After legalizing abortion in 1970, New York State saw more than twenty times more abortions in 1972 than three years before. Also in 1972, the year before the Supreme Court decided *Roe* and abortion was deemed a "constitutional right" in the entire country, the Guttmacher Institute estimates nearly six hundred thousand abortions were performed nationwide. The number jumped dramatically each year. By 1980, the number of abortions skyrocketed to 1.6 million—an annual rate that held steady through the 1990s. The proportion of nonwhite women having abortions increased from 23 percent in 1972 to 44 percent in 1999.[35]

The law on abortion matters incredibly. Yes, it's important to care for the parents of these babies, as we'll talk about more in the next section, but let us not water down the absolutely crucial fight for the *legal* right of these babies not to be killed by arguing that other methods of abortion prevention carry equal weight.

The truth is, even if there were no resources available to women in crisis, even if our government provided no welfare, even if we accepted zero refugees each year, abortion would still be evil. Its legalization would still be wicked. And it would still be righteous and urgent for the Christian to fight against it.

Those who say they're Christians yet believe abortion should be legal follow the same logic of Peter Singer and the eugenicists, though they don't realize it. They've imbibed the dark, depraved, demonic lie that humans in the womb are less people than humans outside the womb. Therefore, they believe, the conversation around murdering them should be "nuanced" and "holistic" rather than straightforward. It's not just cognitive dissonance; it's sin. Those who profess to follow

Jesus yet sit on the side of those who advocate for the legal killing of defenseless image bearers don't just need their minds changed by people like you and me, they need their hearts changed by the Holy Spirit.

They need to understand this debate isn't necessarily about the number of abortions or the circumstances where it's more "justifiable." Empathy tells us only to care about how the pregnant mother is in that moment. Truth and love demand that we recognize without qualification these babies' right to live. Yes, we also want abortion to be unthinkable and therefore rare, but first and foremost, the humanity, value, and rights of these children must be recognized by law so that they can receive the same legal protection that the rest of us have against violence and murder.

Suffice to say, pro-life *is* about abortion—not every other factor that makes life easier to live. It's supposed to be. Abortion is a unique, imminent, tangible threat to innocent human life. Don't let anyone tell you it's wrong to be more concerned with abortion than other political issues. It's literally a matter of life and death. There's nothing else like it in our political and cultural debates, besides perhaps euthanasia. Pro-lifers are absolutely right in prioritizing abortion, including when it comes to how we vote.

And if we want to care for the poor and vulnerable, we don't need to outsource all of our compassion to the state when we are called to take up the mantle of charity ourselves. The model of the early church shows us that Christians were compelled by the Holy Spirit to give up their goods *voluntarily* for the benefit of the church (Acts 2:45). After all, it is a *cheerful* giver God loves, not one who only provides for others when the government forces them to (2 Cor. 9:7). Charity is the responsibility first of the church.

It isn't the government's job to fulfill the God-given role of the church, but it is its job to punish wrongdoing and reward good (Rom.

13:3–4). Therefore, yes, we can and should vote for policies that regard babies in the womb as the people—the image bearers—they are. We should never vote for any politician, left or right, who will advocate for policies that make their murder easier.

There is no perfect political party. Not even close. The Kingdom of God isn't split by Republican and Democrat, red and blue. There are sincere Christians and counterfeit Christians in both parties. But let's just be clear: that does not mean these two choices are morally equivalent.

The current Democratic Party may project empathy, but it openly advocates for a no-limits approach to murdering preborn children. And before you balk at this accusation, I encourage you to try to find a single Democrat who publicly advocates for any kind of abortion limit. There may be a few, but they're extremely rare.

Ultimately, we know, abortion is much bigger than politics. Wins in the political arena that lead to abortion restrictions matter, but never as much as the winning of souls that will lead to a culture of life.

One thing all Christians should agree with: It's truth and love, not fake empathy, that will lead to a true culture of life in our country. And that can be found in the gospel alone.

Grace for the Post-Abortive

For good reason, I've mostly focused on how toxic empathy leads us to ignore the lives of unborn children. They pay the heaviest price in a pro-choice world. Yet ironically, the twisted empathy that makes excuses for aborting a child also urges us to ignore the pain of the women who got abortions. That pain is real and deep. Just listen to Jenny:[36]

I'm twenty-eight years old, and I had my abortion about six years ago. I think about it all the time. I always thought that I'd move past it eventually, but it's only gotten worse. Every time a TV show or program discusses abortions, miscarriages, or sad pregnancy stories, I cry uncontrollably.

The decision for an abortion was emotionally painful, yet I didn't feel like I had a choice at the time. I was with a guy who I knew I wasn't going to end up with. I wasn't in love with him. I was with him because I was lonely, and vice versa. More importantly, I was still in college and I wasn't ready to have a child. So when we found out about my pregnancy, we knew what we had to do.

I cried so hard on the day when the abortion was scheduled that the clinic could not go through with the procedure until a week after the first appointment. If I had realized how much I would regret my decision, I wouldn't have gone through with it. I think about whether it was a boy or girl, what he or she would have looked like, and whether or not he or she would have had my eyes.

These questions tear me apart over and over again. Even though the baby doesn't exist anymore, its brief existence in my womb changed my life forever. I wish I could go back in time and change my own mind. I would hold my newborn child in my arms and never let go.

Jenny's story is gut wrenching. This is exactly what Satan does: He lies, he steals, he destroys. He promises relief from our anxieties and burdens while delivering only pain and sadness.

Every woman who has gotten an abortion and every man who has encouraged the woman whom he impregnated to get an abortion has been deceived by Satan, who loves to trick us into making hasty decisions that lead to lifelong hurt. They've been swindled by the abortion lobby, perhaps by their own friends and family, and even by them-selves. They think their circumstances are understandable, and they'll be able to do this and move on without consequence. But it just doesn't work that way.

Have you had an abortion? Twenty abortions? There is forgiveness for you in Jesus. There is mercy, there is love. There is nothing too big, too much for God to forgive. No one is too far gone, too broken, or too sinful for him to rescue.

In Luke 15, Jesus tells the parable of the prodigal son. A man leaves his father's home and squanders his inheritance, his irresponsi-bility driving him to destitution. He gets a job feeding pigs, and, overwhelmed by loneliness and lack, he finds himself envying the pigs he's caring for.

In a moment of clarity, he realizes his stupidity and decides to return to his father, hoping he'll allow him to serve him as a slave. But the man's father, seeing his son returning on the distant horizon, runs to his son, embraces him, kisses him, and calls his servants to prepare a celebratory feast for his return.

The father in Jesus's story didn't ask his son to clean himself up first. He didn't wince in disgust at how terrible the young man must have looked and smelled after living among pigs. He didn't ask what had happened to the inheritance or how he intended to pay him back. His reaction wasn't frustration or resentment. He looked at his son in love and met his arrival with excitement. "'For this my son was dead, and is alive again; he was lost, and is found.'"

Right now, you may be dead in your sin, but by God's grace, Jesus can make you alive. Right now, you may be an enemy of God, but through Christ, you can become his friend, his daughter. He can make you new. Read Ephesians 2—pray on it, dwell on it. The good news that every Christian has believed in can be good news for you too.

If you've had an abortion, I encourage you to seek the healing only the God who created you can give. A counselor can help you when you call 1-855-771-HELP (4357). Go to your local Bible-preaching church. Talk to someone there. Tell them you need help. There is hope for you, redemption, acceptance, and true love in Christ.

Truth in Love > Empathy

Toxic empathy is a cancer. It is used to pressure women to undergo abortions and to convince everyone else that abortion is okay. It leads to the murder of the smallest, weakest, and most vulnerable children in horrifically gruesome ways. It pulls on our heartstrings through half-baked stories and emotional talking points to persuade women and men that getting rid of their child is the only way out of whatever predicament they are in. And it leaves those same women and men with the wound of knowing deep down that they destroyed a miracle that God had brought to life.

When it comes to abortion, compassion and pity by themselves lead to brokenness and even death. Christians offer something infinitely more valuable: truth and love. Past the headlines and the politics, Christians must relentlessly and lovingly tell and act on the truth of what abortion is, no matter the cost. Yes, we must care for mothers. Yes, we should help struggling families with Christlike charity to the greatest degree possible. But we also must stand firm and declare that abortion is not, has never, and will never be acceptable. That is the only way we can truly love the scared, pregnant mothers who don't know what to do and the beautiful babies they carry. Lives are on the line—and they are worth fighting for.

"Trans Women Are Women"

Even if all is covered by lies, even if all is under their rule, let us resist in the smallest way: Let their rule hold not through me![1]

—ALEKSANDR SOLZHENITSYN

W HEN SHE STARTED TESTOSTERONE, she felt like a weight had been lifted off her shoulders. "Finally," she thought. "I can be me."

I met Laura Perry Smalts in 2023 when she was a guest on my show, *Relatable.* After years of wrestling with her identity, Laura told me she made the decision to transition into a male as a young adult. She'd never been fully comfortable with who she was. Growing up in conservative Oklahoma, she liked things that most boys liked: sports, cars, hanging out with her dad. She never really connected with her mom. She didn't have strong female friendships.

She hated the way being female made her a target of objectification. Laura wanted love from guys growing up, but her relationships in high school and college always resulted in her being used sexually by men rather than respected and valued. She became increasingly convinced that her femininity was a weakness, was the source of her problems and insecurities, and wasn't what she wanted to be.

For years, Laura had an alter ego in her head named "Jake." Jake was strong, confident, and well-loved. Jake was never objectified or used. He was in charge of his life, comfortable in his skin. In her greatest moments of self-loathing, Laura would fantasize about another, more fulfilling life as a man named Jake.

In her late twenties, Laura started dressing as a man. She felt that presenting herself in a masculine way gave her a sense of power and security. But this was the early 2000s, and the word "transgender" wasn't really part of the mainstream lexicon. Laura had to do extensive online research to find a name for what she felt: that she was really meant to be male. Search results came up for a local transgender support group—a rarity in her small hometown. She decided to go to the next meeting.

When she showed up, Laura was immediately met with acceptance and affirmation. The people there, most of whom had the same thoughts about their gender that she did, told her not to even question her desire to be male. "Oh, you're definitely trans," they told her. They didn't even know her name was Laura. To them, she was just Jake.

She felt euphoric, like she was known and loved for who she was deep down. "This," she thought, "will solve my problems."

But she knew she wasn't really a man. To really be a man, she had to look and sound like one; it wasn't enough to wear baggy clothes. Her new friends told her about testosterone treatments. In order to receive them, she had to get a recommendation for a psychologist. She found one who had a reputation for being affirming of patients who wanted to transition genders. Laura booked her first appointment.

In their conversations, Laura shared her feelings, glossing over details about her upbringing and saying the things she knew she needed to say to get approval for cross-sex hormones. She got approval for the cross-sex hormones after just a few weeks.

The testosterone made her feel amazing, both mentally and physically. Laura had dealt with polycystic ovarian syndrome since adolescence, resulting in near-unbearable pain before and during her period. With the hormone therapy, her period eventually disappeared, and with it, her monthly suffering. She was stronger, bigger, more energetic. She felt more alive than she had in years, which she attributed to finally living out her authentic self. Soon she began to see facial hair and noticed her voice dropping in tone, and, as she described it on my podcast, "All these changes at first seemed to be real, seemed to be solving the problem."

She was living her life authentically. She'd found friends, and even a boyfriend, who loved her for who she really was. After so many years of struggle, Laura—now "Jake" to everyone who mattered—was happy.

Liberation or Destruction?

It's hard for most of us to imagine how difficult it would be to feel that we were born in the wrong body. No human being tolerates internal or external chaos well; we naturally seek homeostasis, normalcy, and stability. If an identity change and physical alterations promised to calm the storm ever-waging in our minds, most of us would be tempted to take them.

And so when we hear stories of people like Laura enduring years of struggle, feeling like a prisoner in their own body, we share in their relief when they say they've found peace. Lives like Laura's are no longer rare or novel. We hear similar testimonies constantly from people who say they always felt that there was something wrong with them, and now that they've "transitioned" to the opposite gender, they feel complete. Women "become" men and men "become" women. Trans women really *are* women, we're told. Other times, people claim to be no gender at all, or both genders, or gender-fluid, and how they express their feelings about their identity, they argue, makes them feel free. Our natural, empathetic impulse is to celebrate along with them.

Because their testimonials sound like liberation, who are we to stand in the way? Why should we ever inhibit someone's journey toward healing and authenticity? Isn't the loving, empathy-driven path the one that encourages other people's happiness? And even if we do have some questions or hang-ups about gender transitioning, someone else's decision to change genders doesn't affect us, right? The kindest thing we can do, it seems, is to simply affirm their choices and do whatever it takes to help them live their lives to the fullest. Isn't that what we would want if we were in their shoes?

Plus, we're consistently warned that refusal to accept someone's stated identity can contribute to the chances of them dying by suicide. Who wants to have any part in that kind of harm?

Thus, the empathetic urge to affirm Laura and others like her in their decision to present as the opposite sex is understandable. We want to support any course of action that will ease an individual's inner turmoil.

But ultimately, such empathy-driven affirmation is not just short-sighted, but unloving. The implications of transgenderism go far beyond any one testimony of hurt and healing and into a tangled, dark, and deadly web of ideology, politics, bunk science, bad medicine, and corrupt powers that exploit the pain and confusion of people like Laura, resulting in destruction both for those caught in it as well as the rest of us.

Remember: Love and truth go hand in hand (1 Cor. 13:6), and only the truth can set us free (John 8:32). While the dive we're about to take into the depths of transgenderism is disturbing, it is necessary for us to fully grasp the concept of "gender identity" and therefore to offer truth-filled love to a realm of our modern era completely doused in deception.

Starting Them Young

As a girl, I hated dresses. Frills embarrassed me. My mom, excited to have a daughter after two boys, was disappointed to find that her dreams of endless bows and curls and girly outfits wouldn't be fulfilled in me outside of Christmas and Easter.

My outfit of choice was always a plain white T-shirt and jeans. I enjoyed playing with the boys in my neighborhood. I kind of liked bugs. In the second grade, I developed a weird obsession with snakes. My six-year-old self would have said my favorite movie was *Braveheart*. At ten, my mom finally let me get my hair cut into the super-short bob I'd been wanting forever.

My parents always told me I took after my dad: opinionated, headstrong, decisive. In second grade, the teachers awarded students with "character awards." Since I went to a Christian school, most of these were fruits of the Spirit or in the same vein. The other girls in my class got "friendly," "joyful," "organized," etc. I got "persuasive" and was told I'd make a good attorney. I cried, asking my mom later that night through sobs, "What's an attorney?!"

I wasn't good at school in the same way that a lot of other girls were. While I excelled in the subjects I liked, I was disorganized, couldn't sit still, was relentlessly disengaged from the topics I didn't like, and always questioned the authority my teachers claimed they had.

I had traits that would have been excused or even celebrated in boys, but somehow I knew that they weren't always welcome in girls. That was a struggle I had through high school and even into college: wanting to be accepted and loved as a girl, but always feeling that I didn't fit perfectly into traditional feminine categories. This caused me to pretend to be less assured and opinionated than I was for fear that my personality would make me less appealing or attractive, especially to guys.

I never questioned my gender. I loved being a girl growing up, even while liking some traditionally boyish things, and I never felt discomfort in my body. I still love being a woman today, and thank the Lord, all the characteristics that made me unsure or insecure growing up are now strengths that I utilize and benefit from daily. There wasn't a magical moment for me of coming to terms with the traits God gave me. I matured in my faith in college, found ways to glorify Him through work that suited my strengths, later met a man who loved—and still loves—that I am strong-willed, and became a wife and a mom whose concern is how to honor Christ, not how to fit into superficial definitions of femininity. The snake obsession is long gone, but I still love a good jean-and-tee combo, and I'd accept a "persuasive" award with gratitude.

I can't help but wonder: If I hadn't had such a solid Christian community or if I'd been inundated at school, through friends, or by social media influencers with the kinds of ideas we see today about gender, would I have developed into the woman I am now?

Teens and kids in America today are growing up in a world that tells them sex is assigned by doctors at birth based on the genitalia present, and our gender, or gender identity, is something that's determined by our own feelings. There is no correlation, the idea goes, between sex and gender; they can match or not.

In 2022, Boston Children's Hospital released a series of informational videos about transgenderism in children, articulating these ideas in an effort to support the "transitioning" of adolescents. In one video, psychologist Dr. Kerry McGregor claims children know they're the opposite gender "seemingly from the womb."[2]

The American Academy of Pediatrics (AAP) supports the assertion that children's gender can differ from their sex. In 2018, the AAP published a policy statement that supported the "transition" of minors that includes both the prescription of "puberty blockers," which inhibit the natural process of puberty in the preteen years and can cause sterility,[3] and cross-sex hormones for teens.[4]

The gender-sex separation idea is pervasive beyond the medical community. In honor of "Pride Month," Fox News's *America's Newsroom* aired a glowing feature of a California family whose daughter Ryland's "journey of transitioning," as host Dana Perino described it, started "at age five." Correspondent Bryan Llenas stated that "Ryland" knew she was the opposite sex "before [she] could even speak."[5]

Sex education in American public schools that teaches the existence of "gender identity" is pervasive. For example, California's Newport-Mesa Unified School District employs a sex-ed curriculum that includes the use of the "Genderbread Identity," a childlike depiction of a gingerbread man that attempts to draw a distinction between anatomy and gender.[6] In some school districts, these ideas are taught to students as young as pre-K.[7]

According to journalist Christopher Rufo, over four thousand schools in the United States host gender and sexuality clubs. The stated mission of the national GSA organization is to abolish the American judicial system, as well as "cisgender heterosexual patriarchy."[8] School and public libraries across the country offer books related to gender transition to children, including sexually explicit works like *Lawn Boy* and *Gender Queer*.[9]

In 2023, an elementary school in Missouri allowed a classroom reading of *I Am Jazz* to second graders without parental consent.[10] The book illustrates the story of a boy, Jazz Jennings, whose parents helped him "become" a girl as a child. Jazz Jennings is the star of his own reality TV show on TLC, in which he and his parents detail the complexities of his life, including his surgical transition.

In many schools, not only are students taught that it's possible to reject biology in favor of one's feelings about their gender but teachers and administrators are instructed to lie to parents of students who claim to identify as a gender unaligned with their sex.[11] The state of New Jersey even sued three school districts that chose to inform parents of their children's newly stated identity in an attempt to force the schools to hide such information.[12] California lawmakers proposed a bill in 2023 called AB-957 that could classify parents and entities like churches and schools that choose not to affirm a child's "gender transition" as child abusers, presenting potential criminal penalties for those convicted and stripping parents of custody.[13]

Students can be penalized for refusing to affirm new identities as well. In Wisconsin, a public middle school opened a sexual harassment investigation into three eighth-grade students who failed to call a fellow student "they" or "them."[14] One of the boys' parents explained the new pronouns confused them, as they didn't know how to refer to an individual in plural form.

What is this movement that has so deeply seeped into not just the media and Hollywood but into our education system and children's lives? Is it one driven by compassion for people like Laura, who felt that she'd always been a boy and who found happiness by presenting herself as male?

I have no doubt that many who support the idea of gender fluidity and of presenting it to children do seek to alleviate harm and to protect kids and adults questioning their identity from bullying and discrimination. They want to foster acceptance and love, teaching children from a young age that it's okay not to fit into any box and to live authentically.

So, in that sense, it *is* a movement powered by empathy. But it's a toxic empathy that pushes us not only to have compassion for someone's difficulties but to unquestioningly affirm their feelings, because, if we were in their shoes, we'd want our feelings to be affirmed.

But what about when affirmation causes damage to the very people we say we're loving?

The truth is, this toxic empathy is a dangerous guide for our decisions, behavior, and public policy. What someone wants or feels can't tell us what's morally right or beneficial, either for the person as an individual or for society as a whole. Feelings are often misaligned with reality and can actually blind us from—rather than lead us to—wisdom.

Far from rainbows and liberation, the process of changing the body or even a name, pronouns, and clothing is a serious one, and can be extremely painful, dangerous, and life-threatening to those caught in its clutches . . . like Laura.

The Brutality of "Transition"

Laura looked in the mirror, finally flat-chested. No more compression tops and chest binders. She'd gone through with the "top surgery"—a double mastectomy—and what she hoped would be one of the final steps in her female-to-male transformation. Maybe now she'd finally feel man enough.

But it was just days after the surgery when she realized her hopes for complete masculinity were yet unfulfilled. If anything, she felt less like a man than she had before. Even with a lower voice, facial hair, and a flat chest, she was painfully aware of all the ways she was still a woman. Internally, she still had female parts that she wanted nothing to do with. So, several months later, she underwent a hysterectomy. While she wasn't sure about "bottom surgery"—a phalloplasty, where an artificial form of male genitalia is constructed, typically from forearm skin—because of the complications it could present, she felt confident that removing her uterus and ovaries, which had caused her years of pain due to polycystic ovarian syndrome, would complete her trek to manhood.

But as she recovered from the invasive procedure, Laura found herself more depressed and lost than she'd ever been before, even pretransition. She'd been convinced that changing her name, her pronouns, and her body would make her happy forever. Abandoning her Christian upbringing and cutting out her parents, she believed, would help her become who she was always meant to be: Jake. But she didn't feel like someone who'd completed a heroic journey. She felt like someone who'd lost a game, the rules of which she only now realized she never really understood, after years of believing she was close to victory.

Laura plummeted from the height of euphoria to the depths of despair, from feeling excitement from her new masculine facial features and body composition to wondering how she could possibly live like this forever. Facial hair, a low voice, a flat chest, and broad shoulders belied what she knew would always be true: she was born female.

Her hands, feet, the size of her heart, her lung capacity, and her DNA would never change. She felt like something other than human—not fully woman, not fully man—like some kind of hybrid creature who'd lost her personhood in the pursuit of authenticity. The pain of the problems of her past that she thought would be solved by rejecting her female identity was still present. The rejection she felt from her mother and the betrayal of the men whose love she desperately wanted still stung. "Jake" didn't erase her past, couldn't heal her.

To obtain her testosterone prescription years earlier, she'd been required to meet with a psychologist. Ultimately, the doctor signed off on hormone therapy. But before she did, she put down her pen and notepad, leaned forward, and looked Laura in the eye. "Wow, you really have issues with your mom." Laura bristled, offended at the suggestion that perhaps her discontent was due to other underlying factors rather than being a man trapped in a woman's body. Those words haunted her now, but she still wasn't ready to face them.

The testosterone the psychologist had quickly approved had taken a toll on her female body. Testosterone enlarges the larynx, lowering the voice significantly. Facial hair grows, and head hair often thins. The body's fat composition changes, with more weight collecting in the torso rather than the hips. It also allows for greater muscle growth. For many, these changes are mostly irreversible.

For most women, large doses of testosterone also stop ovulation and menstruation. The consequences of artificially pausing the natural female cycle can include permanent infertility, though the data analyzing the long-term effects is extremely limited. Dr. Maddie Deutsch, the medical director of the Gender Affirming Health Program at the University of California, San Francisco, says that on testosterone "some people may experience mood swings or a worsening of anxiety, depression, or other mental health conditions as a result of the shifts associated with starting a second puberty."[15]

Physically, women on testosterone can expect to experience extreme acne,[16] hair loss, headaches, high blood pressure,[17] and high cholesterol,[18] and are more at risk to develop type 2 diabetes,[19] liver dysfunction, and breast and uterine cancer.[20] Women on testosterone are also more than four times as likely to have a heart attack compared to other women.[21]

Men on cross-sex hormones can face a similar fate: lower muscle mass, erectile dysfunction,[22] infertility, and higher risk of stroke,[23] blood clots, and a host of other potential issues.[24]

The dangers of so-called sex-change surgery are often even more terrifying.

"Bottom surgery" for men means vaginoplasty, where surgeons use penile tissue to create a man-made vagina. The most common technique is a penile inversion procedure, where the penile skin is used to construct the vaginal lining. In some cases, there is not enough skin to achieve the necessary vaginal depth, so surgeons will take a skin graft from the upper hip, lower abdomen, or inner thigh.

During the surgery, the surgeon installs a mold inside the new vaginal canal for a few days to make sure it doesn't collapse. After it's removed, patients need to shove a plastic rod called a dilator up their vagina regularly in the years following surgery to make sure it stays open. If it closes or swells—a common complication since the body interprets the cavity as a wound—patients risk infection and incontinence.

Recovery from a vaginoplasty is brutal: symptoms can include swelling and soreness, phantom pains at the top of the now mangled penis, urethras too swollen to allow urination, and perhaps a lifetime of incontinence and sexual dysfunction requiring even more surgeries to fix.

Phalloplasty is even more dangerous. In these highly dangerous surgeries, surgeons create a penis-like appendage and urethra from tissue somewhere on the body, usually the forearm or thigh. Often the tube created with the rerouted urethra simply doesn't work.

According to recent research, up to half of patients will have urethral stricture, which means that the body cannot expel urine fully or at all. In addition to causing intense pain and discomfort, the inability to empty the bladder can lead to perpetual bladder and urinary tract infections. Often, patients endure complications requiring a catheter to urinate and must have future surgeries. But after multiple failed reconstructive surgeries, patients can require "lifelong perineal urethrostomy," or an additional opening behind the penis-structure where pee can be expelled.[25]

Our bodies were designed in certain ways. No matter how much empathy you have for gender-confused people, rejecting that design comes with a heavy cost.

When you take a step back, it's surreal that we're even talking about things like creating penises out of girls' forearm skins or carving out permanent wounds inside of young boys. Many believe that these "affirmative" responses to transgenderism are driven by nothing more than empathy and the best science. We've already seen how toxic empathy can lead to mutilation. But proponents of transgenderism don't have science on their side either. The truth is, the "science" behind sex transitioning has a decidedly dark, twisted, and harmful history.

The Sickening Roots of Transgender "Treatment"

In many ways, that history started in the late nineteenth and early twentieth centuries with a man named Havelock Ellis—a close friend of birth control advocate Margaret Sanger. Like Sanger, Havelock was an early supporter of the eugenics movement and believed that sexual freedom coupled with birth control could solve modern ills. To explain how this new world would work, he studied human sexuality, including among children.

His theory was that children, and even little babies, had sexual interests, and that people could sometimes have what he called "sexual inversion," or the benign belief that they were the opposite sex. Both these ideas were highly controversial at the time, and they led to strange conclusions. For example, because Havelock thought children were sexualized, he defended pedophilia and was weirdly interested in childhood masturbation.

Ellis's "research" was taken up by a biologist named Alfred Kinsey in the early twentieth century. Kinsey's goal was to overturn society's sexual mores, and he believed just about every person was secretly deeply sexually perverted. Kinsey popularized the idea that sexuality wasn't black or white but existed on a sliding scale. Where Ellis believed that people could believe they were the opposite sex, Kinsey posited that one's sexual attraction fluctuated and could change. To both, old notions about sex and sexuality were being challenged. Also like Ellis, Kinsey believed that even the youngest kids were sexual beings, and as such, Kinsey worked with pedophiles to study orgasms among young boys, writing about how younger children often sobbed and cried during the experience.[26]

However, there was a major difference between the two men. In the late 1800s and early 1900s, Ellis's ideas were controversial. When Kinsey was writing in the mid-twentieth century, he became an international sensation. His books on sex were widely praised, he was on the cover of *Time* magazine in 1953,[27] and he was dubbed the "father of the sexual revolution."[28] As time went on his ideas about deconstructing taboos and sexuality soon got turned to the idea of biological sex itself. If everything is on the table sexually, why not changing sex itself?

One of Kinsey's primary researchers, John Money, picked up where Kinsey left off. In the middle of the twentieth century, Money clarified the earlier "research" by popularizing the idea of "gender" as distinct from sex—that one could have an identity completely separated from one's biology. Money then began conducting sex-change surgeries from his perch at the prestigious Johns Hopkins University.

Like Ellis and Kinsey, Money had a strange interest in pedophilia, supporting the idea that boys aged ten or eleven can have sexual relationships with men in their thirties.[29] Also like Ellis and Kinsey, he believed ideas about gender and sexuality began in early childhood— including that children were born psychologically neither male nor female. Money tested his theory in the tragic and depressing case of the Reimer twins.

In the 1960s, Bruce Reimer, one of the twin boys, had a botched circumcision that mutilated his genitals. On Money's recommendation, his parents decided to raise him as a girl, dressing him in girl's clothes and raising him as "Brenda." It was the perfect case study to see if gender was based completely on nurture and had nothing to do with nature. Years later, Money announced the study was a massive success—Brenda was a happy girl, "her" brother was a happy boy, and gender is fluid.

Except it was all a lie. "Brenda" was never comfortable as a girl. Despite the surgery and hormones, "she" always knew something was wrong. The little boy was obviously masculine and grew up wanting to be a mechanic. He didn't want to play with dolls, hated dresses, and wanted to pee standing up.[30]

Even more terrifying details of Money's experiment emerged later. When Bruce and his twin brother were six years old, Money wanted to test his belief that "childhood sexual rehearsal play" was crucial to shaping a healthy gender identity. He made the two brothers watch pornography and forced them to rehearse what they saw on the screen while he photographed them.

In the end, Bruce's parents couldn't hide the truth. His parents told him at fourteen that he was a boy, and Bruce spent the rest of his life desperately trying to live as a male and reconstruct the male anatomy that had been surgically and hormonally taken away from him. Tragically, Bruce—who changed his name to David because he felt like he was fighting Goliath—took his own life when he was thirty-eight.

Do you notice a theme? The history of transgender treatment isn't built on solid science and empathy. It's built on the eccentric ideas of perverse, powerful men who all had the goal of deconstructing traditional morals to achieve their sexualized vision of how the world should be. Instead of helping kids, these "experts" hurt children by subjecting them to cruel experiments to justify their theories and play out their sick sexual fantasies.

Sadly, little has changed today. If anything, it's gotten worse.

Kids are still in the crosshairs.

The Kids Are Not All Right

The number of children today being sent into the transgender medical buzzsaw is unprecedented.

When John Money was doing sex-change experiments on children in the 1960s and '70s, few people even knew what transgenderism was. As late as 2005, there were only three gender clinics for children in the entire world. The only clinic in the western hemisphere had a scant eighty patients.[31] Of that tiny number of kids, the vast majority were found to grow out of their gender confusion as they hit puberty and adulthood.[32]

Today, the number of gender-confused youth is exploding. There is no central source for data on transgenderism in America, but the numbers we do see are astounding. In a survey of 137 college students in 2021, nearly 4 percent of undergraduates said they did not fit into a traditional male or female framework,[33] somewhere between 2 percent[34] to nearly 10 percent[35] of high school students said in 2018 that they were gender-diverse, and 42,000 young people were diagnosed with gender dysphoria, nearly twice as many as had that identity two years before.[36]

The number of children and teenagers on puberty blockers more than doubled in the five years from 2017 to 2021—and that number is certainly much higher today. Likewise, over 4,200 young people received hormone therapy in 2021, up from less than 2,000 in 2017.[37]

Meanwhile, horrifying medical stories are popping up everywhere. At a Kaiser Permanente facility in California, a thirteen-year-old girl had her healthy breasts removed.[38] A whistleblower named Jamie Reed from a gender clinic in St. Louis reported that clinicians were routinely giving cross-sex hormones to thirteen-year-olds often without ever considering the child's other mental health issues.[39] After years of puberty blockers, a teenager in Texas ended up with osteoporosis.[40] I could fill the rest of the chapter with examples and not cover half of just what's been reported in the news.

Despite these known risks, kids are still signing up for "treatments," even with their parents' permission. Why?

One big reason adults go along with the madness is moral blackmail. When their child comes out as trans, they're immediately asked: "Would you rather have a living son or a dead daughter?"

This is one of the main empathy-driven pressure tactics the transgender movement uses. It's based upon studies purportedly showing that kids who don't medically transition are significantly more likely to commit suicide. If you don't accept the transition, you're complicit in your own child's death, the argument goes.

The problem is, those studies are bunk. Many are paid for by pro-trans groups[41] and have sample sizes that are too small to be statistically significant. Some studies cited by the trans movement actually show the opposite, such as that those on puberty blockers can be *more likely* to commit suicide than those not on blockers.[42]

The Heritage Foundation published a study overturning the idea that cross-sex medical intervention lowers the risk of suicide. To take just one data point, when controlling for other factors, starting in 2010 suicide rates actually rose in states where puberty blockers and cross-sex hormones became easily accessible for minors.[43]

But a big question remains. Where are all these gender-confused kids coming from? We went from having almost no gender dysphoria to creating a rising cohort of confused, sterilized, breastless teenage girls with geriatric skeletons—and the craziness isn't going away.

This significant increase in gender confusion is in large part the result of something researchers call "rapid-onset gender dysphoria," or ROGD. This was a term coined by Dr. Lisa Littman when she noticed something very strange. In the past, gender dysphoria appeared in an extremely small number of mostly boys at a very young age. Now, large numbers of much older adolescents, especially girls, were coming out as transgender despite having no history of gender confusion.[44]

Researchers are trying to figure out all of the root causes of ROGD—when they aren't silenced by the pro-trans mob, that is. But what we do know about it from Dr. Littman's research is very dark. First, most of the kids aren't born with innate gender dysphoria. They adopted a transgender identity much later. Second, gender confusion is largely spreading among friend groups through something called social contagion. Dr. Littman's research showed how kids wanted to be socially accepted, so large portions of groups of mostly teen and preteen girls start "coming out" at the same time.

Likewise, these aren't random kids coming out as trans. The vast majority of those studied by Dr. Littman have a mental health condition, like autism, or have suffered trauma of some sort in their lives, like a bad breakup or their parents' divorce.[45] These are vulnerable kids, and they are the perfect target for an ideology and identity that promises them a new identity, one in which they will finally be happy.

Perhaps most frightening, transgender identity appears to be spread through heavy internet use. On social media, being a normal, heterosexual, and, heaven forbid, white girl often means you are automatically an enemy, an oppressor, and privileged. Trans people, on the other hand, are celebrated and affirmed victims. Not to mention, the internet is filled with pro-trans content and influencers sharing their "happy" transition stories. With almost no voices telling these kids that transgenderism is dangerous and everyone else either celebrating it or being silent, it's no wonder that teens—a group predisposed to be influenced by their peers—adopt this new identity.

Even more insidious is the influence of pornography, which alters the psychology not just of adolescents but adults too. Pornography is extreme and addictive by its nature. Like drugs, as people watch porn, they need bigger and bigger doses to get the same high. For porn addicts, that means it's almost never enough to watch male-female sexual relations. Soon enough, these people are watching porn videos featuring abuse, child rape, or, increasingly, transgenderism.

In 2021, transgenderism was the tenth most watched category on the site Pornhub, with a growth rate of 141 percent from 2020.[46]

Another extremely popular and related category is "sissy porn," where men are humiliated and forced to act and dress like women. As Reduxx reporter Genevieve Gluck told me on *Relatable*, men who were trying to give up porn in general but were specifically addicted to sissy porn said this type of porn was "weapons-grade mind control" because of the extreme element and the way it altered their perception of themselves. Andrew Long Chu, a male who now identifies as a female named Andrea, whose writing on gender won him a Pulitzer Prize, is very vocal about how sissy porn made him trans.[47]

The trans lobby is trying its best to discredit ROGD and Dr. Littman's findings, but there's no other viable explanation for why adolescents with no history of gender confusion are coming out together in social groups. What's worse, those in power—proclaiming their empathy for these kids—celebrate it.

There are many reasons for this: ideology, the drive since the sexual revolution to overturn all sexual norms, false science, and wrong beliefs about the nature of the human body, to name a few. But the transgender craze is also extremely popular because it is making powerful people rich.

The market for sex reassignment surgery in the United States was estimated to be $1.9 billion in 2021 and is expected to reach $5 billion by 2030.[48]

The cost of phalloplasty ranges from $20,000 to $40,000, and the entire "bottom surgery" package can generate up to $100,000 for hospitals.[49] "Chest reconstruction" can cost $40,000 per patient, and vaginoplasty generates at least $20,000,[50] not including the hospital stay, anesthesia, and post-op visits. Increasingly, health insurance is required to cover it all.[51]

Dr. Shayne Sebold Taylor from the Vanderbilt University Medical Center put their support for trans medicine most succinctly: "These surgeries make a lot of money."[52] And that's not to mention that people attempting to trick their body to "become" the opposite sex must regularly pay for hormones, injections, and other pharmaceuticals for the rest of their lives to keep up the charade. To the medical establishment, child transitioners are the best customers of all—they will pay for medical services from puberty to their graves. And if a kid has regret and wants to detranstition? Well, then the medical system can make even more money on more treatments.

Thanks to weaponized empathy, gender-confused people are sent down an expensive, irreversible medical rabbit hole. But they are far from the only people harmed by the lies of transgenderism. All around the country, women's spaces are being violated by men who think they are women.

Hurting All Women

The powers that be tell us ad nauseum that "trans women are women." They want us to have empathy for gender-confused people. But what about empathy for women like Riley Gaines, Hannah Arensman, or Tamikka Brents?

Riley faced off against a male-turned-"female" swimmer at an NCAA championship—after she and other girls were required to change in front of him in the locker room—and was told the male would get to pose with the trophy, undoubtedly because it sent the right political message. Hannah spoke of how terrified she was to have an over-six-foot-tall man run into her during a woman's cycling competition. She quit the sport because she recognized she physically couldn't outcycle a male competitor no matter how hard she trained.[53] And Tamikka was knocked out by a male-to-"female" fighter in an MMA match, left on the ground with a concussion, broken orbital bone, and injuries requiring several staples to her head.[54]

It's not just sports. In Logan Correctional Facility in Illinois, the state's largest women's prison, a female inmate was raped by a gender-confused male. The victim says officials tried to cover it up, and she was punished for reporting the crime because the state wanted to justify its policy of putting men in women's prisons.[55]

A bearded man named Darren Merager entered the women's-only section of Wi Spa in Los Angeles and exposed himself to several women, including a six-year-old girl. The women reported that Merager was aroused, and they were mortified by this violation of their privacy and safety. They reported the incident to the spa, but afterward the media claimed their complaint was based on transphobia, while Merager said he was the real victim of sexual harassment because he's trans.[56]

In Windsor, Canada, a male with visible five-o'clock shadow who renamed himself Desiree Anderson slipped into bed with a woman at a women's shelter and sexually assaulted her. The police posted Anderson's photo and asked for help locating him—but also told people to refer to Anderson as a woman.[57]

This is the predictable result of transgenderism. If we accept that people can change genders—or even if we don't but agree to be "polite" and call a man "she"—then why shouldn't "she" be allowed to play women's sports or bathe naked in an all-women's space? Why shouldn't "she" be allowed to enter women's abuse houses or be transferred to a women's prison? Why accept one lie and not the whole thing? These stories aren't rare. Websites like Reduxx.info post near daily on various ways gender-confused men violate women's spaces.

For that matter, how can we stop "her" from getting puberty blockers, receiving cross-sex hormones, or removing "her" penis? False empathy affirms feelings, and this is what people feel, after all.

Ultimately, there is only one reasonable place to draw the line, and that's at the truth.

Why God Made Us Male and Female

The Bible is explicit from the beginning: "So God created man in his own image, in the image of God he created him; male and female he created them" (Gen. 1:27).

When it comes to gender, we know what the biological and biblical reality is. There is no scientific nor scriptural category for a "gender identity" that is independent from sex. Sex is not a spectrum, and gender is not fluid. While the manifestations of femininity and masculinity vary somewhat from culture to culture, or even between individuals, this variation does not create new identities or sexes. No amount of empathy for confused people can change that.

Further, God created us as male and female so that we could be fruitful and multiply, subdue the earth, and have dominion over it (Gen. 1:28). Here, Scripture provides a teleological view of human nature, which means it shows us the purpose of our biology. We were not given our bodies arbitrarily, but by a God who does everything with intention and purpose.

The secular world teaches that we can do as we please to our bodies without consequence. It says we can have sex with whomever we want and in any way we want, and that we can change, alter, or discard our bodies at will. Ultimately, this false belief about the body is the root of the world's misunderstanding around issues like same-sex relations, euthanasia, abortion, and gender.

Christians reject this view. We know that our bodies are temples of the Holy Spirit (1 Cor. 6:19). Yet even for non-Christians, the body has both temporal and eternal significance. God dictates what bodies we have and how our bodies are supposed to function, and promises to resurrect and redeem the bodies of his faithful without sickness, pain, or decay (1 Cor. 15:42–45).

The prophet Isaiah urges us explicitly to accept the body God gave us: "Woe to him who strives with him who formed him, a pot among earthen pots! Does clay say to him who forms it, 'What are you making?' or 'Your work has no handles'?" (Isa. 45:9).

Christians should never affirm confusion. Instead, we must love people enough to tell them the truth—no matter what some Christians, like Preston Sprinkle, may argue. In a 2022 video, Sprinkle said, "I don't think it's necessarily lying [to use preferred pronouns]. . . . Can we be hospitable even in disagreement, and use their pronouns? And that's the view that I would recommend."[58]

I'm sure that Christians like Sprinkle who use "pronoun politeness" have good intentions. But it is a lie to call someone something other than his or her biological sex. Even more profoundly, using preferred pronouns signifies we think we know better than God. Are we more loving than God, who *is* love? (1 John 4:8). Have we a better idea of mercy than its Giver? (Ps. 55:1). Have we fooled ourselves into thinking we can outcompassion compassion's Source? (Ps. 103:13). Have we so deluded ourselves that we think we care more about lost sheep than the Good Shepherd? (John 10:10–11).

Every Christian would deny these accusations of blasphemy, but every time we use preferred pronouns we are implicitly saying that God, who created the heavens and the earth (Gen. 1:1), does not have authority to define all things—and that he is not *good* to do so. We're saying we are nicer, more merciful, and more compassionate than God.

Just think of Laura. In the end she wasn't saved by preferred pronouns or transition. Grace guided her to redemption—as it does for every believer—through truth, not lies.

We last saw Laura when she was a depressed and anxious physical wreck after years of war against her biology. But her parents never stopped praying for her. While Laura was exchanging her female identity for "Jake," her mom was trading in the legalistic religiosity of years past for a grace-filled understanding of Jesus and the gospel. As God sanctified her, she yearned increasingly for the return and salvation of her daughter. So she and her husband continually asked the Lord to soften Laura's heart and to draw her to Himself.

They refused to call Laura by her male name or pronouns. While they knew this angered their daughter and had the potential to create distance between them, they trusted that standing unwaveringly on the truth honored the Lord and would serve to remind Laura of her true identity.

The lack of affirmation from her parents was frustrating, yet Laura never doubted their love for her. They still insisted on using her birth name, but they didn't push her away. They called, texted, and invited her to visit as often as they could, always telling her how much they cared for her and prayed for her.

While she'd gained plenty of affirming friends and romantic partners through her transition, she couldn't shake the feeling that none of them really knew her, and, therefore, they didn't really love her either. They brushed off her concerns about surgical transition and hormone treatments and simply encouraged her to foster her masculinity.

But Laura wasn't happy as a man. She was so sure transitioning would bring her confidence. Instead, she felt like an impostor. She was haunted by the fear that she'd made an irreversible mistake, that she'd taken a bite of the fruit filled with the promise of Godlike power that came with self-identification. What if her problems didn't really stem from being a "man in a woman's body"?

Without telling her doctor or friends, Laura stopped taking hormones. She slowly started to come to terms with the fact that her womanhood was inescapable. And she started being more responsive to the only people she felt really knew her—the only people in her life who'd refused to call her Jake—her parents.

When Laura's mom asked her to help design a website for a Bible study she'd be leading at church, Laura obliged. Part of the task included transcribing dozens of Bible verses. There was something that pricked her heart as she wrote out the Scripture. Though the feeling was inexplicable to Laura at the time, she felt an uncomfortable pulling that she couldn't describe or ignore.

Over the next few months, she called her mom every day to catch up and ask questions about the Bible. Laura noticed her mom was gracious, patient, and gentle: a contrast from the mother she'd had as a child. Laura sensed that she was softer now, but also more exuberant. Calmer, but more joyful. She knew it had to do with her mom's faith and love for the Bible. Every conversation they'd have, her mom would bring back to Jesus.

She started attending her parents' church—the same church she'd attended as a child—a place she swore she'd never step foot in again. These were conservative Christians, and Laura had convinced herself that because they never affirmed her male identity, they were hateful and ignorant, obstacles in the way of her happiness.

But now she realized that these nonaffirming Christians weren't hateful at all. They'd just seen what she originally couldn't: denying the gender God purposely gave her would only lead to more confusion and desperation. When she returned for the first time, she was met by warm smiles and embraces from her parents' friends. They didn't judge her for her past. They were loving her through it all.

After returning to church and God's Word, Christ saved Laura, showing her the depth of her sin was only outmatched by the depth of His love for her. Even as a Christian, though, Laura still heard the voice in her head that told her she wasn't feminine enough, pretty enough, desirable enough, *whatever* enough to be a woman. But she continued to tell herself something she heard Dr. Everett Piper say on the radio: "We are not made up of our feelings, instincts, and inclinations. Despite our feelings, we can choose our behavior. We are made in the image of God."

Now, Laura lives authentically as the woman God made her and always called her to be. She got married to a Jesus-loving man in 2022 and travels the country sharing about the transformative power of God's grace.

When I met Laura, she radiated a combination of humility and confidence. It took me only minutes of talking to her to realize these are derived from her love for Christ. Her gratitude for His forgiveness is palpable. The godliest people I know are characterized by this same kind of gentle joy.

I love listening to testimonies like Laura's, because it does the Christian heart good to be reminded that, in the midst of the chaos, confusion, and downright evil of our world, God is working faithfully and mightily. He's rescuing lost sheep, finding lost coins, running after prodigal sons and daughters.

Every Christian testimony has one key commonality: someone in their life was brave enough to tell them the uncomfortable truth. Essentially, that uncomfortable truth always boils down to this: "You are living a lie, and the path you're on won't give you the happiness you're seeking. Your sin, which you think is your friend, is actually killing you. That love, purpose, and identity you're seeking—it won't be found in sex, alcohol, your job, your boyfriend, yourself, your gender identity, or any of that. These things can only be found in the God who created you."

That's why there's no excuse for those of us who see the truth to pretend we don't for the sake of "empathy."

Yes, there are well-meaning people who believe supporting transgenderism is loving and virtuous. But they are, whether they know it or not, merely useful idiots.

They enable the chemical castration of young boys, the mutilation of teen girls, the manipulation of autistic youth, the sexualization of children, the violation of women, the mockery of science, the demolition of proper medicine, and the destruction of cohesive society. They sow confusion and induce chaos by perpetuating the lie that it is possible to become the opposite sex.

So, what must we do in contrast? Most importantly, we must tell the truth and never back down from it. We never give in even an inch to the madness. We never declare our pronouns, even when told we must by our employer or professor. We never use a person's pronouns that we know contradict their God-given gender.

We are exceedingly precise in our language, dropping terms like "biological female" to describe a woman masquerading as a man, since that gives credence to the idea that it's possible to be a nonbiological female. We never affirm the claim that everyone who identifies as the opposite sex suffers from gender dysphoria and therefore must be accommodated accordingly.

In other words, we refuse to lie.

You Can't Say You Didn't Know

You can no longer say that you haven't seen the dark underbelly of the trans movement. Whatever horrifying details you've learned in this chapter, the full history, story, and impact of transgenderism are orders of magnitude worse. Just know that there are thousands upon thousands of confused, abused, and mutilated children out there, and there are too many adults ignoring it for the sake of niceness or affirming it for the sake of ideology and profit.

The church must be what it has always been in times of tumult: a beacon of clarity to combat confusion, courage to combat cowardice, and compassion to combat callousness.

With clarity, courage, and compassion, we teach our children the beauty of God's design for gender. We correct our friends who are in error. We admonish our loved ones who are tempted to don fake empathy by affirming lies rather than demonstrating biblical, truthful love. We speak boldly and gently to those we know who have been deceived by transgenderism's lies. We persistently push back against any and all compromise on this issue in our churches, schools, and communities. As we say on my show often: We raise a respectful ruckus.

Empathy for a lie leads to destruction. Telling the truth about transgenderism is the only way to love.

LIE #3

"Love Is Love"

> *There is a way that seems right to a man, but its end is the way to death.*
>
> —PROVERBS 14:12

I AM DEEPLY, FINALLY FINE. Fine through my bones and soul and mind and just every fiber of me."

After struggling for years with drugs, alcohol, depression, and an eating disorder, Glennon Doyle Melton felt free—like she could breathe again. After her vitriolic first marriage ended in divorce, she was now married to the love of her life, a person who felt like home.

Glennon rose to fame over a decade ago through her Christian mom blog, *Momastery*, in which she wrote with shocking honesty about the hardships of marriage and motherhood. Her first book, *Carry On, Warrior*, paints a deeply relatable, redemptive picture of the common difficulties of being a wife and mom. Deemed "the ultimate confessional writer," Glennon's contagious authenticity, courage, and determination had won her an audience of thousands of women who shared her feelings of exhaustion and hope in the midst of life's big and small obstacles.

In 2016, Glennon revealed in her second bestselling memoir, *Love Warrior*, that her husband had been unfaithful. She detailed wrestling with the decision to stay or leave. That same year, Glennon announced her divorce and her new relationship with former U.S. Women's Soccer player Abby Wambach.

They'd met at the *Love Warrior* launch party in Chicago, and both describe a love-at-first-sight moment that felt nearly supernatural.

"Just everything in me was like, there she is. Like just an absolute and total recognizing, even though I've never seen her before," Glennon told the hosts of *What's Her Story with Sam & Amy* in 2020. "I think my heart and my soul knew way, way sooner than my brain," said Abby.

Announcing their relationship on Facebook, Glennon said: "She loves me for all the things I've always wanted to be loved for. She's just my favorite. My person . . . I get it now. I get it. I am in love. And I'm really, deeply happy."

Glennon describes an idyllic situation with her now wife, Abby, her ex-husband, Craig, and their three children. "We have family dinners together. . . . We go to the kids' school parties together. Our children are loved. So loved."

While some longtime Christian followers expressed their shock and disappointment at the announcement of her new relationship, the overwhelming majority celebrated Glennon and Abby. The pair has now grown an audience of millions of female fans, readers, and podcast listeners with their message of self-love and authenticity. Glennon's most recent memoir, *Untamed*, which chronicles her love story with Abby and urges readers to similarly pursue their desires, has sold over two million copies.

The couple's social media pages are characterized by joy and laughter. Their love is obvious. The relationship they've maintained with Glennon's ex-husband is commendable. Abby is a doting, supportive partner, and Glennon remains unapologetically honest and endearing. Their joint lives seem to embody the motto "Love Wins."

Glennon followed her truth, embraced her authentic self, and pursued the life she wanted to live. She insisted that love is just that—love—and it's not limited to any gender or type of family. And now, finally, she's happy. After years of struggle, doubt, addiction, rejection, and pain, she's found peace.

Empathy for Authenticity

Who wouldn't want to celebrate a story like Glennon's?

Glennon's evolution feels liberating. She's found her true self after years of painful self-denial, having been stuck in a miserable marriage with an unfaithful husband. She carried the burden of insecurity and sought to numb her pain through substances and self-harm. Then salvation showed up at an unexpected moment, in an unlikely person: Abby. All of a sudden, it seemed, everything made sense.

She's content; their children are loved. What else matters? We're told that if we really empathized with Glennon's struggle we would affirm her choices, even if we haven't been in her exact circumstances. If we put ourselves in her shoes, we can imagine how wonderful it must have been to feel, after years of brokenness, like her life was finally made whole.

But for Christians, it's not so simple. The inconvenient reality is that we have a priority that's higher than our own or others' momentary happiness, and that's truth. While we can understand Glennon's struggle, our sympathy must submit to our belief in a God who is real and authoritative, and who therefore defines sin, relationships, proper sexuality, and marriage. These definitions all matter, and they matter much more than a person's seeming happiness or authenticity. What's more, only by submitting to the truth as God defines it can we—and those we love—be truly and eternally happy.

But saying as much is hard.

In 2018, I was asked to speak on a panel hosted by the Family Research Council on the definition of marriage. I've always believed that marriage is between a man and a woman, but I was nervous about articulating that stance publicly. Even among conservatives, this is a polarizing position. I'd just started getting booked on Fox News prime-time shows regularly, and I was afraid that being socially conservative may endanger my opportunities there.

I was relieved when another obligation conflicted with the FRC event, but I was also left with guilt over my cowardice on such a clear and basic biblical tenet. If God says it, why should I be embarrassed by it?

Over the next year, it became obvious I had a responsibility to speak clearly on the issue. At the end of 2018, I received several messages asking me to respond to a recent interview in which Christian artist Lauren Daigle said she's unsure whether homosexuality is a sin.

Because of her influence on Christian women, I wanted to rebut her response with biblical truth on my podcast. I could sympathize with Daigle's fear of sounding unloving for calling out sin—I'd just been there myself—but the Holy Spirit had also helped me to realize that the clarity God gives us on this and so many other moral issues is a gift, that we get to receive and to give to others.

I was nervous, and I softened my argument with caveats about the importance of showing kindness toward those whose lives we disapprove of. But my message was this: God is clear that homosexuality is a sin, and the only sexual relationship he calls holy is that between one man and one woman. I addressed the progressive arguments to the contrary and finished with a reminder that all people, no matter their sexual attractions, are called to repentance and self-denial.

As expected, I received a barrage of angry comments and messages accusing me of hate and even insisting I'm not truly Christian. But the grateful messages outnumbered the outraged ones, and I realized just how desperate we all are for clarity on controversial topics. From then on, I've taken every opportunity I can to point to what the Bible says on things like sexuality and gender.

I don't do this because I enjoy controversy or hate people like Glennon, but because these are identity-related issues that have a major impact on how we think of ourselves, others, sin, and God. They matter immensely to our theology, our society, to children, and to human happiness—especially for people with same-sex attraction.

How we define biblical marriage and sexuality affect how we respond to stories like Glennon's: either with affirming but toxic empathy or with truth-filled love.

As difficult as it might be, Christians are always called to choose the latter. And when it comes to marriage, our choices have high stakes.

What Is Marriage For?

In the past, the vast majority understood that traditional marriage was the foundation of a stable society, flourishing children, and, for most people, a happy life. But by 2015, when the Supreme Court decided *Obergefell v. Hodges*, public opinion was changing rapidly. That year, 55 percent supported "gay marriage" and 39 percent opposed (I say "gay marriage" because, as we'll soon see, biblically it's not actually a marriage). By 2019, 61 percent supported and only 31 percent opposed. Today, most people seem to think that restricting marriage to a man and a woman is hateful.

This massive swing in public opinion is unprecedented in human history. Until ten or twenty years ago, very few people in the world would have called a relationship between two people of the same sex a marriage. In 2008, the majority of Americans were opposed to "gay marriage." That same year, when Barack Obama was running for president, he said he didn't support legally redefining marriage at all. A couple of years earlier, then senator Joe Biden had declared matter-of-factly that "marriage is between a man and a woman, and states must respect that."[1]

In 2004, half of Democrats opposed calling same-sex unions "marriage."[2] And it was a Democratic president, Bill Clinton, who signed the Defense of Marriage Act in 1996 that defined marriage in federal law as a union between one man and one woman.[3]

Bill Clinton, Joe Biden, Barack Obama, and the vast majority of Americans weren't extreme for opposing the redefinition of marriage. They simply believed what human beings across the world have known for millennia—that a society has an interest in protecting the special union between a man and a woman, primarily because of its unique ability to produce children. Without this life-giving relationship, no society exists.

In a 2004 debate against Barack Obama for a seat in the U.S. Senate, Alan Keyes gave one of the clearest explanations of the unique procreative function of marriage and America's consequential responsibility to protect it. Though the two candidates agreed at that time on the definition of marriage, it was Keyes who got to offer a response to the argument that male-female relationships aren't special, since many heterosexual couples cannot or do not have children.

Keyes asserted that marriage between a man and a woman is life-producing *in principle*, even if not always in practice, and that is what makes it unique.

The word "in principle" means "relating to the definition of." Not relating to particular circumstances . . . Human beings reason by means of concepts and definitions. We also make laws by means of definitions. . . . An individual who is impotent or another who is infertile does not change the definition of marriage in principle.

Because between a man and a woman in principle procreation is always possible, and it is that possibility which gave rise to the institution of marriage in the first place as a matter of law and governance.

But when it is impossible as between two males or two females, you're talking about something that's not just incidentally impossible, it's impossible in principle. And that means that if you say that that's a marriage, you are saying marriage can be understood in principle apart from procreation.

You have changed its definition in such a way as in fact to destroy the necessity for the institution, since the only reason it has existed in human societies and civilizations was to regulate from a social point of view the obligations and responsibilities attendant upon procreation.[4]

Keyes clarified a point many people ignore: Because the state has an interest in protecting its continued existence and future citizens, it has an interest in protecting marriage. Marriage serves as a bedrock for functioning societies. Upending marriage leads to chaos.

The Centre for Social Justice in the United Kingdom issued a report in 2019 finding that the rise of divorce and single-parent households has led to the destabilization of children's lives. The breakdown of the family nearly doubles a child's chances of failing at school, doubles a child's chances of becoming a criminal, more than doubles a child's chances of becoming homeless, and increases the risk of mental health problems and drug addictions.[5]

Harvard University sociologist Robert Sampson describes the family structure as "one of the strongest, if not the strongest" predictors of violence in the urban United States.[6] This is acutely demonstrated among black Americans, whose communities face a disproportionate amount of violence.[7] In 2018, seventy percent of black babies in the United States were born to unmarried women, far more than any other race in the United States.[8]

Meanwhile, children in a stable, married household have better economic mobility, financial stability, educational achievement, and physical, social, and emotional health.

But it's not enough for children to have two parents—whoever those parents may be. The family diversity myth which posits kids do just as well being raised by any loving adults, is wrong. As Brad Wilcox, a professor of sociology at University of Virginia and fellow at the Institute for Family Studies told me on my podcast, "When you actually look at the data, what you see is that kids are much more likely to be flourishing when they're raised in an intact, biological married family with their own mother and father." In fact, a study by the Department of Health and Human Services found that children living in a home with an unrelated adult were nine times as likely to be emotionally, sexually, or physically abused than kids living with their biological parents.[9]

That hasn't stopped the media and scientific establishment from trying to convince us otherwise. In 2023, *BMJ Global Health* published a study that the media claimed proved kids of homosexual parents fare better than kids of heterosexual parents. *Forbes* covered its release with the headline: "Kids Raised by Same-Sex Parents Fare Same As—or Better Than—Kids of Straight Couples, Research Finds."[10] *The Hill*, *The Washington Post*, and others echoed the same line.

It was a shocking finding—but it also wasn't true. I'll spare you a lengthy explanation of the methodological flaws of the Chinese Communist Party–funded meta-analysis and instead focus on its actual results, which weren't nearly as conclusive as the headlines proclaimed. Suffice to say, two out of five studies in the analysis found children with gay parents suffer more emotional problems than kids with traditional parents. One study showed children with lesbian parents had worse physical health. Likewise, in four of the six studies analyzed, children in gay households had lower graduation rates and worse educational attainment than kids in traditional households and were more likely to repeat grades.[11] But we don't need studies to tell us what we already intuitively know: The same people needed to make a baby are needed to raise her. Only men can be dads, and only women can be moms. Each has their own irreplaceable role to play.

When my kids want adventure and risk, they go to their dad. When they need comfort and sympathy, they come to me. When they want to be chased around the house, they call for him. When they're sick or tired, they cry for me. This isn't due to personality differences but rather our innate gender differences. Moms and dads complement each other in a way that brings security and stability to their kids' lives.

Are there exceptions to these observations? Sure. None of this is to say that all kids who aren't raised by their mom and dad are destined for failure, that there aren't stellar single parents, that same-sex parents don't love their children, or that parenting dynamics can't differ depending on the couple. There are children raised by their mom and dad who face the same challenges as children who aren't. But we shouldn't ignore the data or dismiss our own instincts and experiences when it comes to the need for mothers and fathers.

And we shouldn't support the redefinition of marriage just because it's the popular thing to do. True, it's unlikely that this issue will be relitigated anytime soon. Decades of persuasion through the media and in academia have chipped away at public opinion over time, with a powerful push in the last ten or so years to solidify America's support for same-sex unions. Regardless, Christians should know where we stand and not be mindlessly led by toxic empathy that will destroy the people we are supposed to love.

We may be in the minority, but no poll can ever change what the truth about marriage or the effect redefining it has on children, the most vulnerable and voiceless members of society. Marriage between a man and woman is a child-producing *and* child-protecting institution. "Love is love" may sound like a no-lose slogan in support of "gay marriage," but it undermines and collapses the purpose of the marriage union. When this union is deprioritized or redefined based on the desires or political agendas of adults, children suffer, not just during their upbringing but from their conception.

A Gay New World

In April 2022, *The New York Times* featured a gay couple, Nicholas Maggipinto and Corey Briskin. Their insurance company denied them coverage of IVF and surrogacy. This wouldn't have happened, the men insist, to a heterosexual couple struggling with infertility. So why should it happen to them? If they're a married couple unable to conceive, why shouldn't they receive all the same benefits that a man and woman do?

Their insurance policy made clear that a couple had to try to conceive a child naturally for at least a year to qualify for infertility coverage. But of course, that doesn't apply to Nicholas and Corey. Neither of them suffers from infertility. They can't have a child because gay relations are infertile by nature.

That argument didn't seem to matter to the couple. "It's mind blowing that in 2022 we're still having this conversation about a policy that so clearly excludes gay men because of horribly antiquated views of homosexuality," Corey said. "We got the ability to get married and the rest would have been kind of smooth sailing, but we were sorely mistaken."

In a way, Corey is right. Love is supposed to be fruitful, and for them love is love, after all. And if a couple like Glennon and Abby has kids, why not Nicholas and Corey? If two men have the legal right to be "married," why shouldn't they enjoy the same legal right to have children, complete with all the benefits and access a heterosexual married couple has?

This is a predictable and grave consequence of redefining and rearranging the family. The arrival of "gay marriage" has dramatically impacted how children are created. Since two men or two women can't produce children, the options for starting a family are either adoption or sperm or egg donation. While both choices leave a child without either a mom or a dad, the second route presents far greater ethical concerns.

For two women who want children biologically related to one of them, sperm is required. For two men, eggs are required. The sperm and eggs are considered donated (hence, "sperm/egg donor") in order to abide by America's legal prohibition against selling human tissue. Technically, they're getting paid for their time and effort rather than for their sperm and eggs, but it's obvious what's really being bought: the DNA necessary to make a child.

The prospective parents will pick their sperm or egg donor out of a catalogue. They may employ a service to help them find what they're looking for. They can filter their search by eye and hair color, ethnicity, education, background, and more.

Popular YouTuber Shane Dawson, who once justified pedophilia in a podcast interview, documented his and his partner's journey to becoming parents via egg buying and surrogacy. In the video explaining the process, they joked about which ones will be born and which will be discarded. They laughed at the absurdity of how their children are being conceived: The pair "purchased" the child's mother, fertilized her eggs with their sperm, and created twelve embryos who all have their own bar code.

A lesbian couple going the sperm-buying route will use in vitro fertilization (IVF) to create and carry the child. One of the two women may choose to use her own eggs to mix with the sperm, while the other may choose to be implanted with the embryo, or one of them may play both roles.

With two men, the process requires more steps. After choosing the egg seller, the couple also chooses a surrogate, who will be implanted with the embryo after the egg has been fertilized with the sperm of one of the men. Typically, both the egg seller and the surrogate are strangers, and they're both paid significant fees for their services.

After the baby is born, she's immediately taken from the surrogate and given to her new male caretakers, one of whom is her biological father. She's not only robbed of her biological mother, the egg seller, but she's also separated from the only other person she's ever known. For nine months, she's found sustenance and security in the womb of the woman who carried her. She knows this woman's smell, voice, and heartbeat. This is a powerful, primal bond that's not meant to be broken. We understand this when it comes to puppies and kittens, who we know must be kept with their mothers for eight to twelve weeks after birth, but we've decided that for surrogate babies, it doesn't matter.

Singer Lance Bass and his male partner went through ten egg donors before welcoming his twins, a boy and a girl, via surrogacy. In an interview with Yahoo Life, Bass shared: "The first year, they wouldn't give me any love. They never hugged, they never wanted to snuggle, and I was so upset about it. Because they would do that with my mom. My mom would come over, and boom, they'd snuggle with her."[12] Bass robbed his children of a mother, but that didn't stop their instinctive desire for maternal affection.

Adoptees often speak of what's known as the "primal wound" that they endured when they were separated from their moms as ba-

bies. Some suffer from this wound their whole lives, feeling abandoned and like they don't fit in with friends or family, even if they
have loving adoptive parents.

Even so, adoption is generally redemptive, whereas egg/sperm
selling and surrogacy are not. Adoption has the power to redeem a
broken situation, while these technologies *create* a broken situation.
Adoption helps a life that's already been created, whereas the reproductive methods we've just described *create* a life with the express
intention of taking the child away from its mother or father.

This produces a deep wound that almost unconsciously grows in
children. It did for Ross Johnston. Ross was born via artificial insem-
ination and raised in a home with two lesbian mothers. I had him on
my podcast, and he told me that despite growing up without a dad
and being raised within the homosexual community he could tell something was off.

"Inside . . . I didn't know what the language was or what the
expression was," he said, "but I was longing . . . for a father. I was
longing for somebody who would provide, who would protect."

Ross was only able to put words to what he was feeling when he
turned sixteen and, against all odds, became a Christian. As he came
to know the Lord and His Word, he started to gain the language to
express what he was feeling. "That's why I felt lonely. That's why I felt
anxious. That's why I felt hopeless, because I never had a true father
who actually was able to father me as I was being raised up."

According to Olivia Maurel, children born from surrogacy experience similar trauma. Olivia is a thirty-two-year-old woman who was
born via traditional surrogacy, where the surrogate was also the egg
"donor." She didn't know her birth story while growing up, but she
could always sense something was wrong. She never had a bond with
her "mother," she didn't look like her, and they didn't really share
anything in common. The alienation Olivia experienced from the

woman raising her led to feelings of abandonment, troubled relationships, and addiction to drugs and alcohol.

At first, Olivia wondered if she was adopted. Then, she started
Googling around where she was born and found information about a
surrogacy center. Suddenly it clicked, and it's like she knew.

"I still have that void," she told me. "My mother, biological mother
and surrogate mother, she left me at my birth. She left me. She ex-
changed me for a check. . . . She did abandon me at one point in my
life where I needed her the most, and that left a void. And that void,
I tried to fill it up my entire life."

As a baby she was treated like a transaction—a transaction intentionally designed around a birth mother abandoning her child. And
that trauma doesn't go away, even if the surrogate uses an egg from
the woman who intends to raise the child. No matter what, in surrogacy, a child that has spent nine months intimately bonding with a
woman in gestation is ripped away from that mother when he is born.

"We have the right to know where we come from," Olivia told me.
"We have the right not to be separated from our mothers at birth. We
have the right to be raised by our mothers. And these are just such
primal and important rights that we step on and we just spit on with
surrogacy."

Surrogacy can also be painful for the surrogate. While she may
earn tens of thousands of dollars for renting out her womb, the process is not without its emotional and physical risks.

I interviewed a surrogate on my podcast who carried a baby for
two men. About halfway through her pregnancy with their baby boy,
Brittney, a mother of her own four children, was diagnosed with aggressive cancer.

The gay couple who'd once treated her with love and gratitude
quickly turned on her when she shared her diagnosis. Instead of showing concern, they were angry. They threatened lawsuits and falsely

alleged that the surrogacy service or obstetrician had hidden Brittney's cancer diagnosis. And even when Brittney insisted that she'd be willing to do everything possible to deliver a healthy baby, they were still incensed that she may have to give birth early to a premature baby.

When the doctors told Brittney that it was no longer safe for her to be pregnant, she was at twenty-four weeks gestation. Babies as early as twenty-one weeks have survived outside the womb, so Brittney's hope was to deliver the baby early and allow the doctors to give him the care he needed to survive. But the couple who hired her had other plans.

They were adamant that they didn't want a premature baby. They insisted that she abort their son. "The parents threatened the hospital, they threatened all the doctors if anyone delivered me [that] they were going to be sued. They threatened anybody they possibly could with a lawsuit," Brittney told me. They did everything possible to ensure their baby wouldn't be born alive.

Brittney was desperate for a way out. Her obstetrician helped her line up three different families willing to adopt the baby. Brittney said her sister would have adopted the baby, and she was even willing to adopt him herself.

The couple refused. They demanded that she abort the "fetus" as soon as possible, so they could start the process over with another surrogate.

Brittney was distraught. She wanted so badly to save the little boy she'd felt kicking inside her womb for weeks, but she had little choice, as she had no legal right to make decisions on his behalf. She found a hospital that was willing to deliver the baby. He was born on Father's Day. He lived for a short time. Brittney said, "He was, you know, cared for and loved a little bit. I don't know how much that means to most people, but he was."

As for the "fathers," they never saw the boy. They ordered that his remains be cremated and ended their relationship with Brittney.

While this isn't characteristic of all same-sex surrogacy situations, it's important to know that this reality exists, is completely legal, and is the consequence of redefining marriage as something other than the life-producing union of a man and a woman.

And if you're wondering, yes, I am opposed to these reproductive technologies even for male-female couples, and it's not because I don't feel deeply for people who face obstacles in fulfilling their desire to become parents. Surrogacy and egg/sperm selling always intentionally wound a child by separating them from their biological parent or the woman who carried them. Even IVF carries its own ethical problems, particularly when eugenics are involved and when surplus embryos are indefinitely frozen or trashed. As Christians who understand these are humans made in God's image, we are obligated to care about how these little people are treated.

While I am opposed to practices like egg and sperm donation, IVF, and surrogacy in any circumstance, the context in which these technologies are used does matter. Remember, marriage as an institution exists for the procreation and raising of children. For a heterosexual couple, infertility is circumstantial, but they have the type of love that *could* produce children. On the other hand, infertility in homosexual couples exists, as Alan Keyes would say, in principle—by the very nature of the relationship. That means interventions like IVF and surrogacy are often a last resort for a man and woman trying to have a baby, but they are necessarily a first choice for a same-sex couple who wants to have a baby.

Put another way, opposite-sex couples most often turn to these fertility treatments in desperation for the children their union could, in principle, naturally create, but same-sex couples use these interventions to have children their relationships would never otherwise be able to produce.

We can have empathy for those who desire children, but we cannot accept toxic empathy, which demands that we agree that that pain should be alleviated by whatever means necessary. Instead, we must show true love, which has compassion for a person's desire to be a parent while insisting that children's rights supersede adults' desires.

A Refuge for the Fatherless

The redefinition of marriage is a radical social experiment at the behest of adults and at the expense of children. *All* progressive social experiments require children to make sacrifices: whether it's abortion, gender ideology, race-based DEI education, or shutting down schools for COVID-19. The voiceless and most vulnerable are always made to pay the price.

This is the opposite of humanity's intended order: the strong are supposed to sacrifice on behalf of the weak, not the other way around. As we discussed in the abortion chapter, that's the order that Christianity championed. Rather than exploiting the helpless, we're to honor and lift them up.

One group that God repeatedly commands Christians to honor and uplift is the fatherless. Mistreating fatherless children was forbidden in ancient Israel (Ex. 22:22). God describes Himself as their father and defender (Deut. 10:18; Ps. 68:5). God regards advocating for the fatherless as righteous, and He condemns as wicked exploiting them (Jer. 7:6, Ps. 94:6). Children without fathers are always, without exception, categorized by Scripture as oppressed and in need of special protection.

Yet through the redefinition of marriage and reproductive technology we're creating fatherless children every day—and celebrating it.

We're likewise creating motherless children. The Bible doesn't have much to say on motherlessness, simply because this has never been a widespread phenomenon. Moms are less likely to abandon their children; the biological bond between them is so strong that it's much more difficult to sever than the bond between a father and child. Mothers are predisposed to stick around. And yet, again, by redefining marriage and employing the reproductive industry, we're creating a new tragic trend: motherless babies. It doesn't take much to see that this, like fatherlessness, is a biblical category of oppression for which God has great anger and sadness.

And just as it's been from the inception of the church, the Christian responsibility is to take up the cause of the fatherless—and the motherless. We must advocate for their right to a mother and father. We must defend their dignity from conception onward, refusing to accept a world in which tiny image bearers of God are bought, sold, frozen, and discarded.

Toxic empathy says we must only consider the feelings of adults who want children and affirm their relationship by agreeing with whatever means they choose to fulfill their wants. Biblical love sees the destructive consequences of this affirmation and prioritizes the rights and well-being of the little ones who can't speak up for themselves.

A Portrait of Biblical Marriage

Still Christians may wonder: Natural marriage may be preferred, especially for the sake of children, but does the Bible really reject homosexual conduct and "gay marriage"? Many don't think it does. In 2013, Glennon Doyle wrote, "I know my Jesus, I love Him, and I think if he needed me to believe that homosexuality was a sin, He would have mentioned it."[13]

This is a popular idea: homosexuality isn't a sin because Jesus never said it is.

But this argument is illogical, a misrepresentation of Jesus, and a misunderstanding of Scripture.

It's illogical because the absence of condemnation doesn't equal support. Just because we don't see Jesus mentioning homosexuality by name in the Gospels—just as we don't see him mentioning, say, sex trafficking or torturing animals—doesn't mean he supports it.

It misrepresents Jesus because He is God. Therefore, whatever God says in the Old or New Testament, Jesus says also. Jesus's words aren't limited to what we read in Matthew, Mark, Luke, and John. The entire biblical canon is His, and it's all authoritative and without error (2 Tim. 3:16–17).

The argument also represents a misunderstanding of Scripture. We shouldn't read the Bible asking, "What can I get away with?" Rather, we should ask, "How can I glorify God the most?"

With the former mentality, people try to pick apart pieces of Scripture to see how we can still follow our desires without feeling condemned. But with the latter mentality, we're going to read the Bible with the aim of understanding who God is and how we can best obey Him.

That means we're not only interested in what the Bible says *not to* do but rather in what the Bible says *to* do. We don't just care about what the Bible says is wrong, but what the Bible says is holy and good.

Yes, Scripture does clearly and unequivocally condemn homosexuality as sin, despite baseless claims to the contrary. Leviticus 18:22, 1 Corinthians 6:9, 1 Timothy 1:10, and Romans 1:26–27 all prohibit homosexual relations and condemn them as inherently disordered. But even if these negative verses didn't exist, the Bible's positive definition of holy marriage and sexuality would be sufficient in telling us what Christians should believe and how we must live.

A few years ago, I came up with an alliteration to help me remember why God's definition of marriage as between a man and a woman is so important:

Biblical marriage is *Rooted* in creation; it's *Reiterated* throughout Scripture; it's *Repeated* by Jesus; it's *Representative* of Christ and the church; and therefore it's *Reflective* of the Gospel.

Rooted in Creation. Genesis 1:27 says, "So God created man in His own image, in the image of God He created him; male and female He created them." We see the first marriage in the creation of the parents of all mankind. In this verse we're told what it means to be human, to be male and female, and to be married. God is gracious to provide us with such a clear definition of who we are as people. These were and are the necessary components of all human existence. That biblical marriage is rooted in creation means its definition doesn't change based on the times, trends, or cultural norms. It was purposely made by the God of the universe, who, as its Creator, has the sole authority to define all things.

Reiterated throughout Scripture. Parents and families are defined in terms of fathers, mothers, and children. For example, the first commandment with a promise is "Honor your father and mother" (Ex. 20:12; Eph. 6:2). In Leviticus 19:3, God demands that every member of Israel "shall revere his mother and his father." These are not arbitrary, accidental designations, but rather they speak to God's intentional, good design for the family.

Repeated by Jesus. When Jesus is asked specifically about marriage and divorce, He appeals to the created order to emphasize the sacred definition of marriage and the bond it creates: "Have you not read that He who created them from the beginning made them male and female, and said, 'Therefore a man shall leave his father and his mother and hold fast to his wife, and the two shall become one flesh?'" (Matt. 19:4–5). Jesus affirmed the reality of the gender binary and biblical marriage.

Representative of Christ and the church. In Ephesians 5, Paul explains that the marriage of a man and a woman represents an eternal, spiritual marriage between Jesus Christ and His Bride, the church. Wives, Paul says, are to submit to their husbands as they submit to Christ, and husbands must love their wives as Christ loves the church. Like Jesus, Paul goes back to creation when He speaks of marriage: "Therefore a man shall leave his father and mother and hold fast to his wife, and the two shall become one flesh. This mystery is profound, and I am saying that it refers to Christ and the church" (Eph. 5:31–32). Earthly marriage is a representation of the great heavenly marriage of Jesus and his church, with both the bride and the groom designated with their own particular roles. That's why the redefinition of marriage as anything other than a man and a woman matters so much. Two men or two women can't represent Christ, the groom, and His Bride, the church: only a man and woman can do that. This definition has spiritual, eternal, and gospel significance.

Reflective of the Gospel. The Bible starts with a marriage and ends with a marriage. The first is the marriage between Adam and Eve, and the last is the marriage of Jesus and his bride, the church. Revelation 19 depicts the marriage supper of the Lamb, wherein the whole church fully and finally feasts with our Savior. Christ's marriage to his church is the redemption of the marriage of Adam and Eve that was tarnished by sin at the beginning. That's the gospel. The marriage of a man and a woman, as an earthly metaphor of Christ the Bridegroom and His bride, is meant to reflect this good news.

That's how profound the marriage definition is! There is simply no way to deny this biblical truth as a Christian without denying the authority of Scripture and thus the gospel itself.

The truth is, though, even when we have our theology down, living it out can be tough. When there's a gay person in our lives, like Glennon, searching for happiness and in need of our love and friendship, applying our theology practically can feel tricky.

While empathy asks us to understand their desires, toxic empathy demands that we affirm them, adopting the motto "love is love" as a way to condone any relationship that people can imagine. But that phrase doesn't mean anything. "Love is love" is a circular motto that is therefore open to any and all definitions. If love is just love, then lust can be love, predation can be love, bestiality can be love . . . the possibilities are endless.

Love must have a meaning for "love is love" to make any sense. Thankfully, the Bible gives us one. Yes, God is love, as 1 John 4:8 says, but 1 Corinthians 13:4–7 gives us more details: "Love is patient and kind; love does not envy or boast; it is not arrogant or rude. It does not insist on its own way; it is not irritable or resentful; *it does not rejoice at wrongdoing*, but *rejoices with the truth*. Love bears all things, believes all things, hopes all things, endures all things" (emphasis added).

As always, toxic empathy and truth-filled love are at an impasse. It's a choice between making ourselves and others feel good and doing what *is* truly good.

It's a lie that the only way to show love to a person who identifies as gay is to celebrate their choices and affirm their sexuality. We can—and must—love them by telling them the truth.

This doesn't mean we try to initiate a friendship by confronting them about their sexual sin. That probably won't work. After all, someone who doesn't follow Christ must first repent of their unbelief before they repent of anything else. That means we get to share with them who God is and what He's done for us before we have any conversation about sexuality and identity.

Two stories of transformation demonstrate how powerful this gospel-first approach can be.

True Love in Action

Dr. Christopher Yuan spent his twenties selling drugs in gay night clubs. He'd embraced his sexuality years prior and was pursuing his desires to their fullest. He was raised in a secular home by hardworking Chinese immigrants. When his mother and father told him that they'd become Christians, he thought they'd lost their minds.

He wanted nothing to do with their newfound beliefs. But when his drug dealing landed him in prison, he found himself searching for something deeper. Lying in bed one night, he looked up to see the words "Jeremiah 29:11" written on the ceiling above him. They stuck in his mind. That week, he found a Bible and located the verse, which reads, "'I know the plans I have for you,' declares the Lord. 'Plans to prosper you, and not to harm you. Plans to give you a hope and a future.'"

A hope and a future were the two things Christopher didn't have. So, with nothing else to do, he kept reading the Bible, hoping God would reveal the hope Jeremiah 29:11 had promised, and He did. In a conversation I had with Christopher, he explained, "I had put my identity solely in my sexuality, and God was telling me your identity is not in anything else other than Jesus Christ."

Christopher didn't know it at the time, but the Lord was answering the prayers of his mother, who'd been relentlessly begging for his salvation both before and during his time in prison. She asked that God would do whatever it took to save her son. He answered her prayer.

In the early days of Christopher's faith, he tried to find a way to reconcile his homosexuality with his relationship with Christ. But he'd read the Bible, and he knew as hard as it would be that he couldn't hold on to his sin if he was to follow Jesus.

In his book *Out of a Far Country*, Christopher wrote, "God's faithfulness is proved not by the elimination of hardships but by carrying us through them. Change is not the absence of struggles; change is the freedom to choose holiness in the midst of our struggles. I realized that the ultimate issue has to be that I yearn after God in total surrender and complete obedience."

Christopher underwent a change in identity that included repentance from sexual sin as well as a repudiation of *all* sin. His homosexual sin wasn't his chief obstacle to following Christ; it was that he was a sinner, period. In other words, his biggest problem was everyone's biggest problem: that we are dead in sin apart from Christ and need Him to save us. He needed to understand what we all need to understand: that our identity is not in our sexuality, our success, our relationships, or anything else. These things are not who we are. We are either dead in sin, or alive in Christ (Eph. 2:5). And if the latter, then by grace we are called to deny ourselves, take up our cross, and follow Him (Matt. 16:24).

In *Mere Christianity*, C. S. Lewis puts it like this: "Christ says, 'Give me All. I don't want so much of your time and so much of your money and so much of your work: I want You. I have not come to torment your natural self, but to kill it. No half-measures are any good. . . . Hand over the whole natural self, all the desires which you think innocent as well as the ones you think wicked—the whole outfit. I will give you a new self instead. In fact, I will give you Myself: my own will shall become yours.'"

I can think of few Christians who better emulate this self-sacrifice than Dr. Rosaria Butterfield. Rosaria is a former lesbian feminist activist who was a professor of English and women's studies at Syracuse University. In her words, her job was to "make homosexuality look wholesome." She had a vested interest in doing so, since she'd been in a committed relationship with her partner for years. She wanted equal rights and legitimacy, and she knew this would only be accomplished if enough people affirmed the goodness of relationships like hers. In other words, she was dedicated to securing the public empathy necessary to achieve her progressive political goals.

In Dr. Butterfield's mind, it was a given that Christians were the enemy. With their backward, bigoted views, they stood in the way of equality and liberation.

But then her mind changed—not at once, but over the course of months. Her assumptions about Christians were contradicted by a neighbor who invited Rosaria over for dinner one evening. He was the pastor of a local Presbyterian church, and, she quickly realized, he was anything but hateful. He and his wife were kind, hospitable, and open about their faith in Jesus. They invited Rosaria to dinner again, and she accepted.

Rosaria shared hundreds of meals with her neighbors, and the more she got to know them, the more interested she was in understanding what they believe. She felt the persistent urge to read the Bible for herself, so she did.

And once she started, she didn't stop. The truth was unleashed, and she allowed it to change her. The Holy Spirit took over and, as He always does, began chipping away at her sin, asking her to release her idols. When He got to her lesbian relationship, she didn't want to let go. The pain was understandable: she loved this woman. But, ultimately, she loved Jesus more.

Rosaria took up her cross and followed Christ, thanks to the way God used a loving, truth-speaking, gospel-preaching couple to reach her. They chose biblical love over toxic empathy, trusting that Jesus would reveal Himself to her through their obedience.

Today, Rosaria is a wife and a mom of four. She's written several books and provides resources for Christians navigating the difficult issue of sexual identity. And she has happiness in Christ beyond what she ever could have imagined before.

I first learned of Rosaria's story in 2016, when I came across an article she wrote in response to author Jen Hatmaker's announcement that she is now an "LGBTQ-affirming Christian."

She wrote: "If this were 1999—the year that I was converted and walked away from the woman and lesbian community I loved—instead of 2016, Jen Hatmaker's words about the holiness of LGBT relationships would have flooded into my world like a balm of Gilead. . . . Maybe I wouldn't need to lose everything to have Jesus. Maybe the gospel wouldn't ruin me while I waited, waited, waited for the Lord to build me back up after he convicted me of my sin, and I suffered the consequences. Maybe it would go differently for me than it did for Paul, Daniel, David, and Jeremiah. Maybe Jesus could save me without afflicting me. . . . If I were still in the thick of the battle over the indwelling sin of lesbian desire, Jen's words would have put a millstone around my neck."[14]

Jen opted for toxic empathy instead of truth-filled love, and, as Dr. Butterfield put it, her words served not as a means of liberation but of great burden for those struggling with disordered sexual desire. She was pushing people to embrace the lie that rooting their identity in their sexuality, not in God, is the way to happiness.

But Rosaria reminds the readers of this truly freeing truth: "How I feel does not tell me who I am. Only God can tell me who I am, because he made me and takes care of me."

That article convicted me when I first read it. At that point, I still kept what I considered my *super*-conservative views, like the definition of marriage, fairly quiet. To the world's proclamation that "love is love," I was responding with silence. But her powerful words had planted seeds in my heart that took root and then blossomed years later when I finally made my stance clear publicly.

Rosaria's thoughtful arguments have continued to teach me over the years, not just when it comes to the theology of sexuality but also when it comes to the application of this theology in politics.

While we may be sure of our theological stance on sex and marriage, how do we live this out in how we interact with the nonbelieving world, particularly in the political realm? In other words, is it okay to hold these Christian views while voting in a way that contradicts them?

We know what toxic empathy would say: Support the position that fulfills the desires of those who identify as LGBTQ. But where does truth-filled love lead us?

Personally Against, Politically For?

Until the last few years, I wasn't sure where I stood on the legalization of what's referred to as "gay marriage." While I knew I personally didn't support it, I wasn't sure it was fair for me to oppose its legality.

In an interview with gay conservative commentator Dave Rubin, I articulated my view on marriage and sexuality. To his credit, Rubin was extremely respectful of my view. But he said he drew the line at

Christians like me opposing his legal right to be married to a man. That was and is a popular perspective, even on the right side of the aisle: while we can be personally opposed, we must be publicly supportive.

I would have aligned with that position at one point, or I at least wouldn't have been able to argue the opposing opinion. Several years ago, pastor and author Tim Keller assured Christians that it's possible to "believe homosexuality is a sin and still believe that same-sex marriage should be legal." While Keller himself didn't hold that position, his assurance of this possible "middle way" between full-on affirmation and total condemnation of gay relationships gave room for Christians like me to take the position more acceptable to the non-Christian world.

But my view has changed. I realized over time that the "privately against, but publicly for" stance doesn't make much sense. If I believe that God is the Creator and Authority over all things, and if I believe that His ways are better than ours, it's illogical to support institutionalizing sin.

The law can permit sin, but Christians should not accept laws that approve of or are designed to make it easier to sin. Put another way, it's one thing for the law to allow same-sex attracted people to live with each other and even form lives together. In America we have a great degree of respect for freedom, even the freedom of people to do that which is wrong. That, and Christianity allows for a large diversity of political arrangements (Matt. 22:21). But it's another thing for the state to call "marriage" that which God declares is not marriage. Then the state isn't just allowing error, it is promoting and defending it—and making it easier for people to turn their backs on God.

Practically balancing freedom and support for biblical truths is difficult, and something Christians have had to negotiate since Jesus founded the church. But at a bare minimum, as Christians we should always desire our human law to conform with God's divine law.

On my show, Rosaria Butterfield explained, "It is never in a Christian's interest as someone who is to love your neighbor as yourself to put a law between a fellow image bearer and a holy God that would prevent her from coming to Christ." She urged Christians who supported *Obergefell*, the Supreme Court decision to legally recognize same-sex unions, to repent. She views it as an obstacle for gay people to repent by making it easier for them to sin. She's thankful she wasn't legally married when she became a Christian, as the disentangling from her partner would have been much more burdensome.

As people who believe in God's total authority and goodness, we should always seek to vote in a way that aligns with our worldview. To do so isn't scary "Christian nationalism" or "fascism," as critics of conservative Christians say. It's just doing what everyone else has a right to do in America: bringing your moral beliefs to the voting booth. Everyone's worldview influences how they vote. Christians have just as much a right and responsibility to support policies that align with what we believe is right as anyone else. If we believe God's ways are good and if we love our neighbors, we will support policies that promote righteousness, biblical justice, and order.

There are good-faith discussions and debates among Christians on what this looks like on each issue. But when it comes to marriage, there's a lot on the line. It's not just that legally redefining marriage as between two men or two women is unbiblical, such a redefinition has serious, practical ramifications for society.

No one explains this better than Professor Nancy Pearcey in her book *Love Thy Body*: "Every social practice is the expression of fundamental assumptions about what it means to be human. When a society accepts, endorses, and approves the practice, it implicitly commits itself to the accompanying worldview. And all the more so if those practices are enshrined in law. The law functions as a teacher, educating people on what society considers to be morally acceptable. If America accepts abortion, euthanasia, gender-free marriage, and transgender policies, in the process it will absorb the worldview that justifies those practices—a two-story fragmentation of the human being that denigrates the body and biological bonds such as the family. And the dehumanizing consequences will reach into every aspect of our communal life."

Twenty years ago, her words would have read as a fear-mongering slippery-slope fallacy. But we've quickly learned just how true they are.

And when Christians contradict this dehumanizing worldview, we face rabid opposition and fierce accusations. Indeed, for defending the family we should expect to experience intense blowback and even serious persecution.

"Bake the Cake, Bigot"

Jack Phillips is the owner of Masterpiece Cakeshop in Colorado. In 2012, he told a gay couple he couldn't create a cake celebrating their same-sex wedding. He was happy to bake any other kind of cake for them, but he just couldn't create something that expressed approval of that which God calls sin.

The next decade of Jack's life was consumed by legal battles. The gay couple who'd requested the cake sued Jack and won.[15] Eventually, Jack and his representation, Alliance Defending Freedom, found themselves in the Supreme Court arguing for Jack's First Amendment right to create art that aligns with his beliefs. They won in a narrow ruling that sidestepped the substance of the case, the justices finding that Colorado had demonstrated anti-Christian malice in their treatment of Jack in court.

Sadly, Jack's legal troubles aren't finished. While the Supreme Court was reviewing the first case, an attorney called Jack asking for a cake that was blue on the outside and pink on the inside to celebrate transgenderism. Again, Jack said no.[16] As I'm writing this, Jack is still fighting for his faith in court.[17]

When I first learned about Jack's legal battles several years ago, I started a GoFundMe for him, which, thanks to the generosity of thousands of donors, raised over $70,000. His business had suffered greatly as he'd been forced to dedicate so much of his energy to the lawsuit. He sent me an email thanking me, and I didn't think much of it after that.

A few years later I got to meet Jack at an event where we were both speaking. We were backstage, and it was almost his turn to take the podium. I quickly introduced myself, hoping to just get a quick hello before he walked onstage. But when I reached out my hand, he stopped, stood up straight, and looked at me. I saw his expression change and his eyes fill with tears. He grabbed my hand and said, "Thank you. The donations from that GoFundMe helped keep my business afloat at a time when I thought I couldn't keep going. Thank you."

That's what we call sharing arrows. I didn't do anything but share a link to a fundraising page, and most people who contributed only donated a little. But through all of these small acts of solidarity, we made a big difference in Jack's life. That's what Christians do. We share arrows with our brothers and sisters when they're in the line of fire.

Because whether we like it or not, one day the arrows will be pointed toward us. It may be one or it may be a thousand, but if we are faithful in defending God's design for marriage and the family, we will catch heat, and perhaps even suffer great loss because of our stance. It may be painful, but it should also be expected. Joy-filled hardship is the normal state of the Christian life. Second Timothy 3:12 promises that "all who desire to live a godly life in Christ Jesus will be persecuted." When the day comes, we'll want others to share arrows with us just as we did for them.

Ultimately, bearing one another's burdens is at the heart of Christianity. It's what Christ did for us on the cross. And it's what Paul directs us to do for one another (Gal. 6:2). That's what true love is—choosing to suffer for the benefit of someone else. And that is deeper and more life-giving than any empty slogan like "love is love" or empathy-driven affirmation of someone's preferences.

Love Isn't Simply Love

It's easy to see a post on Instagram of a beautiful, happy gay couple and feel the urge to applaud their relationship. When someone tells us that they feel free, that they're finally living as their authentic selves, and that everything has fallen into place for them, of course our inclination is celebration.

We *should* want good things for people. We want those we love to feel joy and fulfillment. And they may indeed find forms of these things in their same-sex relationships. But as Christians we must make the effort to think beyond the compelling love story and remember that there are serious theological and societal ramifications of redefining marriage.

We must remember that God's ways are better. If we trust that God is love, that He is good and trustworthy and wise, then we will believe Him when He tells us that the creation of man and woman in the bonds of marriage is "very good" (Gen. 1:31) and when He calls every other kind of sexual relationship unholy. We won't use empathy to affirm what God calls sin. We certainly won't celebrate it. We will only celebrate what God calls good.

That being said, Glennon Doyle was right about one thing: Love does win. But her definition of love is incorrect. LGBTQ activists repeat the circular, meaningless mantra "love is love" as a way to elevate passions that will never ultimately satisfy them. The love to which Christians are called rejoices in truth and goodness as God defines them, because we know that His ways lead to true satisfaction for an individual and order for a society.

This kind of love requires sacrificing our preferences, our desires, and, yes, our sins. But God will not be outdone in generosity (Luke 6:38). Just ask Christopher Yuan, Ross Johnston, and Rosaria Butterfield. They aren't praised like Glennon Doyle. But they chose the love of Jesus Christ above everything else. And they know that whatever they had to give up for the sake of Jesus, God is more, God is better, and God is enough.

LIE #4

"No Human Is Illegal"

Love for one's country means chiefly love for people who have a good deal in common with oneself.[1]

—C. S. LEWIS

MARIBEL TRUJILLO DIAZ WAS afraid.[2] She was afraid for her four children, including her three-year-old daughter, who suffers from epilepsy. She was afraid for her husband, who was suffering from medical issues that left him unable to work. She was afraid for herself, unsure how she could possibly survive being separated from her family, forced to live in a country unfamiliar to her now.

She was afraid because she faced deportation.

The Washington Post was the first to share her story. Maribel and her husband had come to the United States by crossing the border illegally in 2002. Back in her native Mexico, they regularly faced the threat of violence, extortion, or even kidnapping. In America, they hoped for a better future than they could ever have in Mexico. Since then, Maribel found what she was looking for, building a good, quiet life with her family in Fairfield, Ohio. This was their home, their community, the place they loved raising their children. After escaping the threat of violence and a lack of economic opportunity in Mexico, Maribel was grateful for the blessings America had brought her.

Then one day, she was robbed of everything she knew and loved.

She was standing outside a family member's house when they arrested her. Without warning, they transported Maribel to a detention facility without any of her belongings or documentation. She had no idea when or if she'd see her family again. She fretted thinking about her children, who would come home from school and learn their mother was gone and may not be back. She never got to hug them or say goodbye. When would she see them again? What would happen to her baby girl? Maribel was one of the only people who knew how to care for her when she had a seizure. What would they tell her when she cried out for Mama?

Maribel had interacted with immigration authorities before, but she'd never faced deportation. She was confident that if she kept her head down, worked hard for her family, and contributed positively to her community, she could avoid trouble. Even so, she desperately wanted to be here legally. She applied for asylum a few years after she'd arrived in the United States but was denied. In 2014, in a meeting with Immigration and Customs Enforcement (ICE), she was told that she could stay in America as long as she checked in with authorities every year. She agreed. Then, in 2016, she was finally issued a yearlong work permit.

But when Donald Trump became president, ICE began cracking down on people in the United States illegally. Before her year was up, Maribel was next on their list.

After her arrest, she was sent to a detention facility in Louisiana and then deported her to where her parents and brother lived in Michoacán, Mexico, a hotbed of gang violence.

Unable to hug and kiss her children, she spoke with them every night via video chat from her parents' home. Her oldest, Oswaldo, tried to stay strong. With his father unable to work, he wanted to step up to provide for the family. Maribel admired his maturity but knew he was secretly struggling. Her little one, Daniella, didn't understand why she could only talk to her mommy over the phone. One day she made her parents bed up and proudly told her mom on the phone. "When are you going to get home to go to sleep?" she asked. "God will bring you back to me soon." Every word broke Maribel's heart.

Meanwhile, Maribel constantly worried her husband would be deported too. Her children were granted American citizenship since they were born in the United States, but could they remain in Ohio with both of their parents trapped in Mexico? Would they have to join her in Michoacán? If that happened, everything she had struggled and sacrificed for would have been for nothing. She couldn't think about it.

With little hope, all Maribel could do was pray. Every day she prayed "for a miracle," begging God for a way to be reunited with her children.

Mercy for the Sojourner

There are few worse nightmares a mother can endure than being ripped from her children.

Honestly, it's difficult for me to see the justification for Maribel's deportation. She was a responsible community member and loving mother. She's not a criminal. She just did what every one of us would have done: fled violence for the opportunity of a better life. Now, four children are without their mom. We know whom her deportation harmed, but who did it help?

And who can blame Maribel for coming to America for a better life? Most of us who were born and raised in the United States can't imagine the poverty and fear of violence that many women and children endure in parts of Mexico and South America. If we had the chance to find safety and opportunity elsewhere, to build a stable life for our children, wouldn't we take it?

Maribel isn't alone in her experience. There are millions of illegal immigrants living in the United States, many of them with stories like hers. They're hardworking people with jobs and families and friends. They attend church, serve their communities, and help their neighbors. They came here the only way they thought they could, eager for a future without constant violence and economic despair.

And, most importantly, they're people made in God's image. That fact alone means these people have great worth and must be treated with dignity and respect. Plus, God seems to pay particular attention to the plight of sojourners. In ancient Israel, he prohibited His people from mistreating them (Ex. 22:21).

We could stop there, allowing empathy for situations like Maribel's to lead us. That's what outlets like *The Washington Post* want us to do when they publish stories like hers. The more loving thing to do, it seems, would be to advocate for them to stay. Deportation seems cruel. No human is illegal, they tell us. Turning people away at the border who are desperate for a better, safer life feels malicious, un-Christlike even.

But, as always, there's another side of the immigration debate that requires thoughtfulness and biblical wisdom. Empathy can help us feel for the difficult plight of immigrants, but it can't give us the discernment to advocate for good immigration policy. To do that, we have to understand what's really going on.

Who Gets Our Empathy?

"Help me, Daddy!"

This was Kate Steinle's last plea before she died on July 1, 2015.

Moments earlier, thirty-two-year-old Kate, her dad, and a friend had been strolling down Pier 14 in the Embarcadero district of San

Francisco. Out of nowhere, a stranger shot a gun. The bullet hit Kate in the back, piercing her heart. Her dad desperately performed CPR as Kate screamed in pain before losing consciousness. He held Kate's limp body, begging her to hang on. She died in the hospital two hours later.[3]

Authorities quickly arrested the killer and booked him into San Francisco County Jail on suspicion of murder. But two years later, despite ample evidence and eyewitness testimony, Kate's killer was acquitted of all murder and involuntary manslaughter charges.[4]

His name was Juan Lopez-Sanchez, an illegal immigrant from Mexico. Despite having been deported five times and having seven prior felony convictions, Lopez-Sanchez was living safely in San Francisco, which had recently declared itself a sanctuary city for illegal immigrants.

Only a few months before Kate's murder, ICE issued a detainer for Lopez-Sanchez. According to the *Los Angeles Times*, "as the date neared for him to be released into ICE custody, prison officials in Victorville shipped him north to the San Francisco Sheriff's Department on an outstanding drug-related warrant despite an immigration detainer. The San Francisco district attorney's office declined to prosecute what authorities said was a decade-old marijuana possession case, and Sanchez was released April 15."

After Lopez-Sanchez arrived in San Francisco, ICE issued another detainer request. They asked that they be notified before his release from jail so they could take him into custody. The request was ignored.

Sanctuary cities earn their name for largely refusing to comply with ICE's immigration orders. In 2013, San Francisco passed its Due Process for All ordinance, which prohibits authorities from holding immigrants for ICE if they had no violent felonies on their record. Though Lopez-Sanchez had committed several felonies, none of them were violent. So, in spring of 2015, he was a free man. And a few months later, he murdered Kate Steinle in the prime of her life.

Kate's story isn't unique. In 2018, University of Iowa student Mollie Tibbetts disappeared after leaving for a jog. She was kidnapped and brutally murdered by Cristhian Rivera, an illegal immigrant from Mexico. He is currently serving a life sentence.

In 2021, fifty-six-year-old America Thayer was beaten with an eight-pound dumbbell then decapitated with a machete by her boyfriend, Alexis Saborit. An illegal immigrant from Cuba, he'd already been convicted of domestic assault in 2017. Saborit's lawyers argued he was mentally incompetent to stand trial, but the judge didn't buy it. She argued that "the defendant's actions in fleeing the scene, disposing of the murder weapon and other evidence in separate locations, and changing his clothing show the defendant's consciousness of guilt."[5] And yet, in 2023, Saborit was declared not guilty of Thayer's murder due to "mental illness."[6]

In his statement to the court, Thayer's son, Charles, described the years of abuse his mother had endured at the hands of Saborit. His testimony wasn't enough.

Devastated by the ruling, he lamented, "It is tough to understand how somebody can commit cold-blooded murder, plan to do it, tell everyone they're going to do it, have a motive to do it, and then somehow be considered insane."

In 2024, nursing student Laken Riley was brutally murdered by an illegal alien from Venezuela while on her morning jog in Athens, Georgia. Athens is one of three sanctuary cities in the state of Georgia. In the State of the Union in March of that year, President Biden accidentally referred to Riley's murderer as an "illegal" rather than the politically correct term, "undocumented immigrant." Democrats and liberal media pundits spent the next few days chastising the president for using rude terminology to describe the man who ruthlessly murdered a young woman. In an MSNBC interview, Biden said he regretted using the word.

Sadly, this is just a sampling of the lives lost due to crimes committed by illegal immigrants. While some may dismiss these stories by pointing out that citizens also commit heinous murders, the point is that, unlike crimes committed by citizens, every crime committed by a person here illegally is *preventable*. They are all carried out by people who, had strict immigration law been enforced, would never have been here in the first place.

So what do we do with an immigration system that brings us stories like Maribel's, as well as those of Kate and others?

Toxic empathy demands our empathy only go one direction—toward the party the progressive worldview deems oppressed. When they say "no human is illegal," what they're really saying is every illegal immigrant is like Maribel and borders shouldn't stop such people from living in America. But the reality is, there are people on both sides of the immigration debate that deserve our compassion. There is pain felt and loss endured by both citizens and those here illegally.

That's why empathy, even in its best form, isn't a sufficient determinant of right and wrong, nor is it an adequate driver of policy. There will always be hurt people on all sides of any issue. Stories like Maribel's and Kate's matter, but they alone can't give us a full picture of immigration in the United States, and therefore they're not sufficient in helping us think through this issue and its related policies. We have to determine what is actually *true*.

And the truth is, the danger of illegal immigration goes far beyond a few anecdotes of murder. It causes problems for both American citizens and the immigrants themselves.

What the Numbers Say

In fiscal year 2023, Border Patrol recorded 1,254 illegal immigrants convicted of assault, battery, or domestic violence, 2,493 convicted for driving under the influence, and 2,055 for illegal drug possession and trafficking—and that's just those arrested, tried, and convicted.[7] This data doesn't count any of the criminals who got away or who weren't prosecuted thanks to the noncompliance policies of sanctuary cities.

In fiscal year 2021, Border Patrol made nearly 1.7 million apprehensions of illegal immigrants, the largest number ever recorded.[8] That is more illegal immigrants entering in one year than the urban population of any single city in America except for New York, Los Angeles, and Chicago.[9] It's enough people to replace the population of New Hampshire, Maine, Rhode Island, or that of seven other states.[10]

Border Patrol estimates that another two million immigrants crossed the border illegally and got away, though there is no way they could know for sure, in large part due to the sheer volume of immigrants. The Department of Homeland Security estimates that an even larger number—four million—crossed the border in that same fiscal year, 2021.[11] If that level of illegal immigration stayed steady for President Biden's term alone, in just four years more illegal immigrants would have entered the country than the population of forty-six states.[12]

These numbers are impossible to grasp. We are adding entire states' worth of people, many of whom have never interacted with immigration or border authorities.

And these aren't only Mexican immigrants or seasonal workers. According to the Pew Research Center, even as criminal border crossings surged, Mexicans accounted for only 39 percent of the illegal immigrant population in America as of 2021, the smallest share on record. Instead of Mexican immigrants, during the years from 2017 to 2021 we saw a spike of 70,000 more illegal border crossers from Africa living in America, 40,000 more from the Middle East, 200,000 more from Asia, 505,000 more from South America, and 250,000 more from Central America.[13] Mind you, those are just estimates of the numbers *living in America* at that time, it doesn't count the unprecedented increase in asylum seekers or the additional border crossers we've seen since then. Not to mention, these numbers can't be 100 percent accurate, since by definition we can't know exactly how many people have illegally entered our country.

While good data is hard to find, you can't help but notice that the hordes of people on our southern border are almost all young, military-age men. Statistically, in any society that is a dangerous demographic. But because of the sheer numbers arriving, we have no ability to judge the intentions or backgrounds of these young, unattached men.

What we do know is that in fiscal year 2023, Border Patrol caught 160 illegal immigrants on the terrorist watch list compared to 100 in 2022. In 2019, 280 potential terrorists were caught crossing the border.[14]

Meanwhile, Border Patrol encounters too many illegal crossers to detain most for more than a few days, meaning large numbers of immigrants are simply released into the interior of the United States. When keeping so many immigrants in custody for such a brief period of time, Border Patrol is unable to vet them all. As of 2020, there were fewer than twenty thousand Border Patrol agents, many of whom are patrolling the border rather than checking the backgrounds of detained immigrants.[15] The simple fact is, we have no way of knowing how many terrorists, traffickers, or other criminals have infiltrated the United States.

But it's certainly no small amount. From 2016 to 2020, nearly 750 members of MS-13—a notoriously vicious and violent gang from El Salvador—were charged with federal crimes. Between 74 percent and 90 percent of those gang members were here illegally.[16] That means up to 675 members from a single gang committed crimes that never should have occurred.

Americans living in the border towns of California, Texas, and Arizona, many of them immigrants themselves, have been forced to sacrifice the safety of their families and security of their property to accommodate the presence of human smugglers (also known as coyotes) and immigrants crossing the border.

For example, Uvalde, Texas, has become a hot spot of police chases, car crashes, and break-ins.[17] South Texas ranchers have lost property and livestock to border-crossing trespassers.[18] Warren Cude, who raises sheep and cattle in Fort Stockton, Texas, testified before the Texas Senate, explaining: "We deal with damage caused by criminals, trespassers, and traffickers trying to escape law enforcement on an almost daily basis," he said. "Farmers and ranchers must pay for the damages that are caused by this criminal activity, and the costs associated with the repairs can add up quickly."[19]

The danger of illegal immigration isn't just about illegal immigrants themselves, but also the consequences of having a border that is easily crossed. Deadly drugs, weapons, and sex slaves are trafficked by cartels, and smugglers are exploiting the porous border, with great cost to human lives.

The vast majority of fentanyl in the United States is smuggled across the Mexican border, thanks to a sinister partnership between Mexican cartels and the Chinese Communist Party. Vanda Felbab-Brown, a senior fellow at the Brookings Institution told Congress in March 2023: "Chinese actors have come to play an increasing role in laundering money for Mexican cartels, including the principal distributors of fentanyl to the United States—the Sinaloa Cartel and Cartel Jalisco Nueva Generación (CJNG)."[20] In 2022, 73,654 people died from a fentanyl overdose. This number has skyrocketed since 2013, with deaths increasing dramatically every year for the past ten years.[21]

These tragedies include children. A two-year-old in Akron, Ohio, died from fentanyl in 2022.[22] That same year, a one-year-old in Baton Rouge, Louisiana, died from the same cause.[23] A ten-month-old was taken to the hospital after coming into contact with fentanyl on the ground at a park in San Francisco.[24]

None of these crimes should have happened. While some activists argue illegal aliens are less likely to commit crimes, we really have no way of knowing that since they are, by definition, undocumented and there are so many kinds of people entering every day. The important point is this: every incident of theft, assault, rape, manslaughter, and murder committed by an illegal immigrant equals an innocent victim who could have been protected by enforcement of stringent immigration laws.

Illegal immigration can cost lives, and it can also cost livelihoods. The massive importation of immigrants who have few skills has hurt the American worker, especially those who are in a low-income bracket. Harvard economics professor George Borjas argues, "Because a disproportionate percentage of immigrants have few skills, it is low-skilled American workers, including many blacks and Hispanics, who have suffered most from this wage dip. The monetary loss is sizable." The winners are big businesses, because "immigration redistributes wealth from those who compete with immigrants to those who use immigrants." He offered one of many examples: "A decade ago, Crider Inc., a chicken processing plant in Georgia, was raided by immigration agents, and 75 percent of its workforce vanished over a single weekend. Shortly after, Crider placed an ad in the local newspaper announcing job openings at *higher* wages."[25]

Without space and resources to provide to an unlimited influx of people, cities like New York are displacing their own population to make room for illegal immigrants. Ninety-five-year-old veteran Frank Tammaro said he was given a month and a half to find a new home after his New York City nursing facility was sold to house illegal immigrants.[26] The city's homeless shelters are unable to adequately serve the homeless population because of the overflow of poor illegal immigrants in need of help.

This is the unnecessary, preventable cost of loose immigration policy that allows illegal crossings and visa overstays. These are the destructive consequences of failing to secure our border.

At one point, not too long ago, both sides of the political aisle shared similar views on this. The conversation about illegal immigration wasn't centered on empathy for those immigrants but on what's best for the country.

What happened?

A Change of Heart

In 2003, in a TV interview, Hillary Clinton stated, "I am, you know, adamantly against illegal immigrants."[27] In 2005, then senator Barack Obama said, "We simply cannot allow people to pour into the United States undetected, undocumented, unchecked, and circumventing the line of people who are waiting patiently, diligently, and lawfully to become immigrants into this country."[28] And when President Biden was a senator in 2008, he bragged that he had voted for a border fence and argued that the government needed to punish American employers who hire illegal immigrants.[29]

Obama and Biden teamed up to win the White House in 2008. Over the next eight years, they helped earn President Obama the nickname "Deporter-in-Chief" because of his relentless deportation of illegal immigrants.[30]

In 2009, Democratic senator Chuck Schumer told *The Washington Post*, "Illegal immigration is wrong—plain and simple."[31] Senator Schumer's sentiment reflected that of most Republicans and Democrats at the time. While parties have long disagreed on how best to reform our immigration system, both sides agreed on the problem of illegal immigration until recently.

When Trump entered the presidential race in 2015, he ran on stopping illegal immigration, which he claimed made America less safe and hurt American workers. He complained about the drugs and the crime that cross the southern border, and he vowed to build a wall to inhibit the illegal flow of immigrants.

The accusations of racism and bigotry were immediate and intense. The media and Democratic politicians called Trump xenophobic, a tyrant, and a white supremacist. The Democrats' tune on immigration has been shifting further left in recent years, but now it was shifting even more dramatically as a response to Trump.

In a now infamous and clearly staged photo shoot on the border during the Trump administration in 2019, socialist superstar Representative Alexandria Ocasio-Cortez said she "saw with my own eyes that the America I love was becoming a nation that steals refugee children from their parents."[32]

Then U.S. representative for Texas's 16th congressional district Beto O'Rourke called President Trump a "racist" and "dehumanizer" who "has been very clear about who he prefers to be in this country and who he literally wants to keep out with walls and cages and militarization and torture and cruelty."[33]

Actress Alyssa Milano called the border wall "a symbol" of "white supremacy."[34]

Now, it's difficult to find a single Democrat willing to condemn illegal immigration. In fact, most appear to welcome it. In the 2016 presidential campaign, Hillary Clinton supported policies to provide driver's licenses to illegal immigrants.[35] When president, Barack Obama supported mass amnesty by granting blanket citizenship to millions of illegal immigrants.[36] The 2020 Biden for President campaign said that Donald Trump's policies to detain and deport illegal immigrants is "extreme, racist, [and] cruel."[37]

Chuck Schumer had supported a wall for years—even sponsoring a bill in 2013 to strengthen and repair physical barriers on the border. But when Trump asked for a wall, Schumer said, "If you want to open the government, you must abandon the wall, plain and simple." He added that funding for a wall "will never pass the Senate—not today, not next week, not next year."[38]

In the first days of his administration, President Biden moved to overturn as many of President Trump's immigration policies as possible, including increasing the number of refugees America accepts, ending COVID-19 limits on immigration, reducing vetting requirements for immigrants, increasing taxpayer-funded benefits for immigrants, reducing enforcement of immigration law, and stopping construction of the wall, among other policies.[39] His administration fought every effort by Texas to secure the border, removing razor wire and buoys the state had installed to mitigate illegal crossings.[40] According to the Center for Immigration Studies, in 2023 the Biden administration flew 320,000 illegal aliens to 43 different airports in the U.S.—all funded by the American taxpayer.[41]

President Biden and the Democrats signaled to the world that America's doors were wide open for anyone to come in, so it's no wonder illegal immigrants caravanning to the U.S. border have told reporters that they want Biden to do what he "promised" and let them in,[42] or that they believe Biden will give them "free passage across the border."[43]

But in many ways, the tide is turning. While a recent Gallup poll found 68 percent of Americans believed immigration is a good thing for our country, 72 percent said they want immigration levels either capped or decreased.[44] A separate poll from 2022 by NPR/Ipsos found over half of Americans believe there is an "invasion" of illegal immigrants at our southern border.[45] The situation is so bad that in 2023 even President Biden contradicted one of his major campaign promises and announced he would restart construction on the border walls.[46]

Our leaders have done everything they can to embrace and even incentivize illegal immigration, but the American people are turning on it—and it's not hard to see why.

Bad for Everyone

When immigrants know they can easily cross the border with little consequence, they're incentivized to make a dangerous trek from their home country to the United States.

In 2022, John Modlin, the chief patrol agent of the U.S. Border Patrol's Tucson Sector, said that agents had found a four-month-old infant and an eighteen-month-old alone in the Sonoran Desert, abandoned by their smugglers. The same week, Border Patrol pulled two children and a baby out of the Rio Grande. The children died, and the baby was in critical condition.[47]

In 2023, Axios reported the story of Juan, his wife, Jhosnnielyz, and their two small children, who trekked to America from Venezuela. While trekking through the Darién Gap they were robbed and had their IDs torn to shreds by their attackers. Three of the women in their group were raped.[48]

Luis Manuel Matos Alcantra traveled from the Dominican Republic to the Arizona border with the hope of crossing illegally. On his way, his bus was hijacked by a Mexican cartel, and every passenger was robbed. Luis managed to escape, running for his life and leaving several of his friends to an unknown fate. Barely clothed by the time he'd made it through the brush, Luis nearly froze to death on his journey.[49]

PBS chronicled the plight of a fourteen-year-old immigrant referred to only as "L" in the article. Her parents had already made it into the United States, and she was trying to do the same by crossing the border illegally. The group's coyote—the cartel name for those who guide immigrants across the border—allegedly raped her while other men watched and did nothing.[50]

Stories of the rape of women and girls by cartels and coyotes is tragically common, though the vast majority go unreported. In the same PBS report, a woman and her daughter who couldn't keep up with their coyote were offered a deal: let him rape her daughter, and he would help them make it. The mother refused, and the coyote left them in the desert. The only reason she and her daughter survived was because they were found by Border Patrol.[51]

In a report from May 2017, Doctors Without Borders found that nearly one in three immigrant women were sexually abused as they traveled through Mexico.[52] Rape is so routine on the immigrant journey that women are urged to take birth control just in case.[53]

Very often, coyotes and other members of cartels are responsible for these assaults. This highlights an important reality: just because our border is open doesn't mean it is uncontrolled. While there are U.S. authorities at our border, unfortunately, our laws largely prohibit them from taking any action that would deter illegal crossings. In most cases, they are only authorized to manage the flow, not to stop it. That means the United States isn't in charge of our own border; the cartels are.

Right now, the border is essentially a battle zone between cartels like Sinaloa and Los Zetas. The groups are in a murderous war to take over various regions along the border, terrorizing both immigrants and American and Mexican citizens. When cartels control a region of the border, they are able to ensure that only their paying customers (illegal immigrants) are able to cross there.[54]

According to *The New York Times*, smuggling immigrants and drugs across the border has become a multibillion-dollar organized crime business.[55] The cartels' reign of extortion, robbery, rape, and murder is entirely enabled by our lack of border enforcement.

Not only do immigrants experience danger on their way to the States, but they also leave their countries of origin worse off. Mass migration causes what's called "brain drain" in poor countries: the most productive and brightest individuals leave behind the weakest and neediest, exacerbating the dismal state of their home countries.[56]

We don't have the pages to outline potential solutions for the dangerous and decaying state of many of the nations from which immigrants journey to the American border. The reasons for their slow economies and violent streets are manifold: government corruption and exploitation by other, more powerful countries are just two.

But we don't have to have all the answers for other nations to care about our own borders. We don't have to fix the rest of the world before we secure our own country. We can have compassion for the plight of immigrants without advocating for liberal border policy that endangers our own citizens and incentivizes trafficking.

Nations need strong borders to keep their citizens safe. "Strong borders" means a border that's nonporous: one that's guarded by impenetrable structures and armed guards who are authorized to protect their nation against smugglers, drug lords, and traffickers. Strict immigration policy that enforces laws against both illegal entry and illegal presence disincentivizes bad actors from exploiting the border and infiltrating the United States.

Illegal immigration isn't compassionate. We can feel for people like Maribel while still keeping in mind the big picture. Sure, no human is illegal—whatever that means. But humans do illegal things, and mass illegal immigration enabled and encouraged by our leaders wreaks unnecessary and preventable havoc on our nation.

There's no such thing as a perfect policy. Every lawmaking decision has pros and cons, risks and benefits. Where there is strict immigration law, there will be heartrending stories like Maribel's. Where there is loose immigration law, there will be tragic stories like Kate's.

It's unpopular to say, and empathy mongers may refuse to face it, but borders exist for our *good*. They are crucial in protecting a country's citizens and retaining national sovereignty. And with or without these proven risks of illegal immigration, every country has *the right* to enforce immigration law, deport noncitizens, and strongly secure its borders.

This is a principle that's vital to understanding the "why" behind inhibiting illegal immigration.

No Nation Without Borders

After eighteen years of waiting, John and Beatrice had finally become citizens. John had come from Kenya, and Beatrice from Zimbabwe, on student visas to pursue higher education. The two met at the University of Nebraska, where they fell in love. They got married after graduation and in the following years welcomed three sons. John became an architect, and Beatrice put her accounting degree to work before choosing to stay home with her boys.

"We give glory to God for this dream that seemed like it would never come true. Relief, joy, pride, peace, a sense of belonging—we felt all this and more the day we received our citizenship," said Beatrice.

They were diligent in keeping their documentation up to date, which was often a burdensome task. But the relief they experienced when they were granted citizenship in 2020 was worth the work and the wait. They voted in their first election that November, overwhelmed with gratitude for the right and privilege to make their voice heard in the nation they call home.

John, Beatrice, and their boys are some of my family's favorite people. They've enriched our lives beyond what I could articulate here, as they've been an example to us of diligence, kindness, and godliness. They love Jesus and America, and anyone would be blessed to have them as their neighbors, friends, coworkers, fellow churchgoers, or community members.

There's no question that legal immigration allows people into our country who offer incredible contributions to our culture, economy, and overall health as a nation. America not only accepts more legal immigrants than every other country each year,[57] we also have the largest foreign-born population of any nation. In fact, the United States is home to more immigrants than live in the next four top countries combined. To put it another way, America only has 5 percent of the world's population, but we are home to 20 percent of the world's immigrants.[58]

America is exceedingly welcoming of immigrants, but we also retain the right to decide which immigrants come to our country. For better and for worse, immigrants, especially in large numbers, change a country. If a million American immigrants moved to Nairobi, Nairobi would become less like Nairobi and more like America. It should be up to Kenyan citizens to decide if this is a kind of change they want. The same should be true for citizens of the United States.

While America accepts vastly more immigrants in total numbers than other nations, countries like Germany, Austria, and Sweden now have larger number of immigrants as a share of their populations.[59] The cultural conflicts between immigrants and their European hosts are now playing out in the public square.

For example, in the German city of Cologne on New Year's Eve 2015, roughly two thousand Arab and North African men sexually assaulted twelve hundred German women in the streets.[60] One teenage victim in the attack was raped in the middle of the city's main plaza and found herself pregnant. The vast majority of the criminals were generously let into Germany as asylum seekers.[61] That same night, there were also reports of mass sexual assaults in the German cities of Hamburg, Dusseldorf, Frankfurt, Stuttgart, and Weil am Rhein.

In Sweden—before, a quiet, peaceful country—bombings and hand-grenade attacks have become commonplace, including in the capital city of Stockholm. In 2022, there were 90 bomb attacks. From January to mid-October 2023, there were 134 bombings.[62] Why the rise of vicious, terrorist-style attacks? Gang feuds within a vast immigrant population.[63]

We can already see these conflicts playing out in America. In October 2023, after the terrorist group Hamas launched a brutal surprise attack against Israel, taking hostages while raping and murdering innocent civilians, an extremely troubling scene occurred right here at home. Supporters of Hamas held public rallies in New York, Chicago, Fort Lauderdale, and other U.S. cities.[64] It doesn't matter how people feel about the Israeli-Palestinian conflict. What was terrifying is that large numbers of people in America publicly supported a terrorist group that was, at the very same time, posting videos online of its members raping, mutilating, and killing civilians. By allowing mass migration, we allowed the worst passions of one of the most grotesque, centuries-old conflicts into our country.

The entire purpose of the American government is to protect America and Americans. That is its number one job. As long as we have unchecked illegal immigration that undermines our sovereignty, our safety, and our culture, the government is failing at its job.

While immigrants can be incredibly beneficial to a society, it is not immoral for a country to limit the number of immigrants, refugees, and asylum seekers it accepts. A nation's government has an interest in prioritizing the well-being of its own people by being selective in who gains entry. This is a key part in protecting a country's sovereignty, which is its ability to govern its own defined territory and control its own affairs. Without sovereignty, a country isn't really a country.

Every nation has this right to sovereignty. Sovereignty is legitimacy. A nation's legitimacy is necessary to enact and enforce laws, which represent the rights of a country's citizenry.

If a country has no borders, it has no sovereignty. If it has no sovereignty, it has no legitimacy. If a country has no legitimacy, it has no authority to create laws. If it has no laws, chaos ensues, rights are lost, and citizenship means nothing. A country without any meaningful citizenship isn't a country at all.

Every sovereign nation must have the right to enforce immigration policy that protects its citizens and their rights. In fact, it is not only its right to do so, but its responsibility. No nation's government, no matter how rich and powerful, has the capacity to care for every person on the planet or represent all of their competing interests. The most it can do is seek the welfare and interests of its own people.

For America, sovereignty is essential not only to our existence and legitimacy as a nation, but our identity as a people, because here the people rule. Who we allow into our country, legally or not, is at the core of our sovereignty, because if you change who is in America, you change how America is governed. That's the natural result of a system based on elections, representation, and public opinion. This kind of change is not necessarily a bad thing. Different groups of immigrants have added much to our nation. But we have to acknowledge that changes within the population alter the direction of our country.

Some people call ideas about sovereignty "nationalism," and there's much fear surrounding the "nationalist" label because of the progressive attempt to link it inextricably with white supremacy and fascism. But nationalism in its truest sense means placing the needs and interests of one's own nation over the needs and interests of other countries. This is necessary and good. It's a concept most seem to understand when it comes to other nations: People agree that Zambia, for example, has the right to protect its citizens, but when one asserts that America has the same right, they're met with accusations of bigotry. America has this right and responsibility just as any other nation does.

Countries are like families. As parents, the needs of our own children are paramount. We seek to keep them safe and help to meet their needs. This doesn't mean we don't want these things for the children of other families. It doesn't mean we hate our neighbors or view ourselves as inherently superior. It doesn't preclude us from helping those in need or being hospitable to visitors.

But it does mean that we will be careful about whom we allow into our homes and how long we allow them to stay. If they pose a threat to our family, we'll kick them out. We won't invite strangers to sleep in our children's beds, eat our children's food, and wear our children's clothes while our own children go without. That wouldn't be virtuous; it would be cruel and irresponsible.

We love our family more than other families, not because all other families are bad, but because they're not ours. It's okay to prefer our own family's way of life. Families share a name, values, priorities, and traditions. It is natural and right to want to preserve these. So it should be with countries.

In *The Four Loves*, C. S. Lewis describes a healthy patriotism as a love for a people with many things in common, like language, clothes, and institutions. He argues that this love, while seemingly superficial, is good, "because any natural help towards our spiritual duty of loving is good."[65] He goes on to quote his fellow British writer G. K. Chesterton: "A man's reasons for not wanting his country to be ruled by foreigners are very like his reasons for not wanting his house to be burned down; because he could not even begin to enumerate all the things he would miss."

Lewis argues that love of one's own country, like love of one own's family, along with its customs and traditions, is a natural, good love that God has placed in all of us and that serves a spiritual purpose, which is to prime us for the unnatural love to which Christians are called: the selfless love that we show toward individuals that we don't know or even like.

Neither Lewis nor Chesterton is making an anti-immigrant argument but rather they are pointing to the virtue of instinctive loves, like love for one's home. This flies in the face of the popular narrative of our day, which says it is bigoted to love America more than other nations and racist to show concern about the massive and swift importation of people who, in many cases, have no regard for our laws and no intention of assimilating into American culture.

This idea is both modern and Western. We've been fed a steady diet of guilt over the past few decades that has convinced us via toxic empathy that in order to be kind and compassionate, we must believe that America and America alone has no right to prefer our values and our culture over others. Because of America's sins, we hear, we must repent by way of helping people from other countries at the expense of our own.

Such absurd arguments ignore the fact that America is not alone in our sins, but we stand apart in our triumphs. Virtually every nation on earth has a history of conquest, slavery, and injustice. This is the history of the world. America is unique, however, in what we've accomplished in the way of equality of opportunity, equal justice, freedom, and prosperity. While there may be plenty to criticize, especially when it comes to the moral state of America today, there's also a lot to be grateful for and a lot to preserve and protect.

In his book *What I Saw in America*, Chesterton observed: "America is the only nation in the world that is founded on a creed. That creed is set forth with dogmatic and even theological lucidity in the Declaration of Independence. . . . It enunciates that all men are equal in their claim to justice, that governments exist to give them that justice, and that their authority is for that reason just."[66]

Chesterton articulates well the special beauty of the United States, which has been made available to people of all classes and ethnicities but must be carefully preserved through the protection of our nation's sovereignty and a collective commitment to uphold these ideals.

This pursuit isn't just practically and philosophically wise, but biblical.

A God of Order

Some Christians who oppose stricter immigration laws argue that the Bible orders us to love the foreigner. But God's command to love the foreigner or sojourner must be understood against the backdrop of God's character: namely, His orderliness.

Scripture indeed contains several verses about respecting and loving the "sojourner" and the "foreigner." Leviticus 19:34 calls on the nation of Israel to "treat the stranger who sojourns with you as the native among you, and you shall love him as yourself for you were strangers in the land of Egypt." Deuteronomy 10:18–19 tells us that

God "loves the sojourner" and that therefore Israel should love the sojourner too.

These verses are important, and they tell us about the character of God: that He has compassion for the outcast, for the displaced, and the lonely. But any attempt to use these passages as evidence that the Bible demands allowing both illegal and legal immigration is faulty.

First, it should be noted that many, particularly progressives, who use these passages as support for liberal immigration policy regularly criticize Christian conservatives for using Scripture as support for our own policies, condemning us as tyrannical theocrats. But it's not only okay but reasonable and right, for a Christian to allow God's Word to shape what we think about policies and how we vote. We just have to make sure we're doing so properly, through thoughtful exegesis and application. That means we must seek to understand the context.

When Christian conservatives use Psalm 139:15–16, for example, which says that God carefully, fearfully, and wonderfully knit us together in our mothers' wombs, as our reason to oppose abortion, we're not taking the verse out of context. That's what Scripture says, and that's what it means: God made us in the womb, therefore we have human dignity in the womb.

But when progressives use these Old Testament verses as a prescription for unlimited immigration, either legal or illegal, they completely disregard the historical and biblical context of the command to honor the foreigner.

When God called on the Israelites to "love the sojourner," that wasn't a green light for every immigrant to enter Israel—or America, for that matter. Let's look at the context: Just before the Jews left their slavery in Egypt, in the earliest days of Mosaic law, the Lord told his people that the relationship between them and the sojourner wasn't one-sided. Yes, they were supposed to love the sojourner and treat him with respect, but the sojourner had duties too. They had to follow the exact same Mosaic law as the Jews (Ex. 12:49).

In Exodus 12:48, God told Moses that the stranger "shall be as a native of the land" but only if he "let all his males be circumcised." God wasn't condoning uncontrolled immigration, but rather the orderly acceptance of people willing to observe Jewish practices and to assimilate into Jewish culture. Just because aliens wanted to enter into Israel didn't mean that the Jews were obligated to suspend the enforcement of their laws. Reciprocity and respect were requisite. Israel had to respect foreigners and treat them with dignity, but foreigners had to do the same to the nation of Israel, and they could not respect Israel without respecting its laws.

So if we're going to apply the immigration laws of ancient Israel to the United States, we're looking at much more restrictive policies than we have today.

America is not ancient Israel, though, so Christians don't have the responsibility to enact Old Testament laws here. But Christians can and should look at both the Old and New Testaments to learn what actions create a just, peaceful society and what actions enable injustice and chaos.

Of foremost importance in approaching immigration from a biblical perspective is to consider the character of God. He cares for the sojourner, yes, but He is also the Creator of order—"For God is not a God of confusion, but of peace" (1 Cor. 14:33). We see this in the beginning: God creates the universe in an orderly fashion, putting everything in its place with its proper name. To Adam, God delegates the responsibility to name the animals. He creates distinctions between day and night, plants and animals, male and female. God gave genders, marriage, family, language, laws, customs, and traditions that brought order to His people and still bring order in many ways today.

Order is a blessing, while disorder is a curse. God's punishment for the men building the Tower of Babel, for example, was to confuse their languages, thereby creating chaos (Gen. 11:1–9). The apostle Paul expressed fear that he would find the church in Corinth in sin and disorder (2 Cor. 12:20). James warns that "disorder and every vile practice" are the result of "jealousy and selfish ambition" (Jam. 3:16). Another word for anarchy is lawlessness, which is always used negatively in Scripture (Matt. 7:23; Rom. 6:19; 2 Thess. 2:3). Satan is the agent of such disorder and lawlessness. That was his first action as the great tempter: to disorder God's relationship with man by convincing Eve to become "like God, knowing good and evil" by eating the forbidden fruit (Gen. 3:5). On the other hand, God blesses His children by ordering our footsteps and bringing order to nations (Ps. 119:105; Dan. 2:21; Ps. 22:28; Rom. 13:1–2).

Scripture depicts walls, both literally and metaphorically, as a defense against disorder and evil.

Nehemiah called upon his fellow Israelites to "build the wall of Jerusalem, that we may no longer suffer derision" (Neh. 2:17). When the wall was finally built, Levites came to "celebrate the dedication with gladness, with thanksgivings, and with singing, with cymbals, harps and lyres" (Neh. 12:27).

In the Psalms, David calls upon the Lord to "build up the walls of Jerusalem" (Ps. 51:18) and prayed that peace would exist within the walls of Jerusalem and security within her towers (Ps. 122:6–7).

Solomon admitted the necessity of walls when he wrote that "a man without self-control is like a city broken into and left without walls" (Prov. 25:28).

The prophet Isaiah compared the salvation of God to "walls and bulwarks" (Isa. 26:1) and that when the Jews live in a land without devastation or destruction, "you shall call your walls Salvation and your gates Praise" (Isa. 60:18).

I'm not offering these passages as precise policy prescriptions for

American immigration law, but I do hope to demonstrate how highly God regards order, peace, and security for nations, and that walls— or any form of strong borders—are representative of them.

In short, borders create order, while borderlessness creates disorder. Chaos and disorder always have victims, and they're usually those with the least physical, economic, or political power to defend themselves.

It is because of—not in spite of—God's heart for the vulnerable that He gave us the ideas of nations, borders, governments, and laws. Acts 17:26–27 says, "And [God] made from one man every nation of mankind to live on all the face of the earth, having determined allotted periods and the boundaries of their dwelling place, that they should seek God, and perhaps feel their way toward him and find him." Contrary to popular opinion, borders aren't an evil construct devised by tyrants. They're a concept contrived by God.

And yet, not everyone in the church agrees that we should restrict illegal immigration. In fact, some argue that to do so is against our call as Christians.

Where's Our Citizenship?

At the Southern Baptist Convention's Evangelicals for Life conference in 2019, Pastor Afshin Ziafat stated, "America is not our home. It is our temporary home as citizens, but we are only sojourners passing through. . . . Our home is the Kingdom of God."[67] Pastor Ziafat went on to argue that because our true home is in heaven, we shouldn't spend our time thinking about building walls on the border, but instead getting people behind the wall on the border into heaven.

While a leader in the Southern Baptist Convention, Russell Moore chastised Donald Trump for casting "light on the darkness of pent-up nativism and bigotry all over the country" through his immigration rhetoric and policies. Jesus, Moore said, is "a dark-skinned, Aramaic-speaking 'foreigner' who is probably not all that impressed by chants of 'Make America great again.'"⁶⁸

Other Christians argue that we do a disservice both to our country and our church by enforcing immigration law. *Christianity Today*'s editorial board once warned President Trump: "Don't deport our next generation of church leaders."⁶⁹

This isn't a new argument. Matthew Soerens from the National Association of Evangelicals and Daniel Darling from the Southwestern Baptist Theological Seminary wrote in 2012 that evangelicals should seize "the missional opportunity that God has foreordained in the movement of peoples across borders."⁷⁰

Pastor and author David Platt has expressed concern over the church's attitude toward immigration. "It's troubling how Christians in our country are the most resistant to refugees in our community when God is bringing people from places where they have never heard the Gospel right outside our doorsteps. We should be the most wide open to love them. We can reach the nations right in front of us."⁷¹

There are bits of truth in each of these statements. True, we are pilgrims on Earth and our citizenship is in Heaven (1 Pet. 2:11; Phil. 3:20). While we're here, we're tasked with making disciples of all nations, and that's made easier when the nations show up on our shore (Matt. 28:19). It's true that Jesus wasn't a white, Republican American. It's also true that there's a chance the deportation of illegal immigrants could include someone who would have been a leader at a church.

But these statements don't paint the full picture, and they wrongly imply that people who favor limiting immigration, either legal or illegal, are un-Christlike.

First, let's clarify the difference between an immigrant and a refugee or asylum seeker. Out of the millions of immigrants illegally crossing into America, very few are true refugees or asylum seekers. U.S. law is explicit: refugees are those who have a "well-founded fear of persecution due to their race, membership in a particular social group, political opinion, religion, or national order."[72] Not only that, but applicants must first apply for refugee status outside America in a neighboring country. An asylum seeker must meet the "refugee" definition and must be seeking admission at a port of entry of the United States. A person leaving an impoverished or less-developed country for a more prosperous one doesn't qualify as a refugee or asylum seeker.

Second, it's important that these Christian critics of immigration law enforcement get specific: How many must America accept to be considered Christlike? Ten million? A billion? More? Are there any limits or restrictions for which a Christian can advocate without being condemned as unloving? Do we have the right to express any concern about who's entering into our country, from where, or how many? Or is the Christian position really that we must have no borders, lose our sovereignty, and forgo our ability to protect the rights and well-being of our own citizens?

And if there is a limit, what is an acceptable way to enforce it? Anytime illegal immigration mitigation efforts are even suggested, they solicit outrage from many evangelicals. Whether it's a wall, horse patrols, buoys, or barbed wire, much of Christian social media roars with complaints about the cruelty of these strategies when they're implemented.

My perspective is this: America, just like every other country, neither has the capacity nor the obligation to allow everyone in who wants to enter. It cannot be one nation's responsibility to take in the world's impoverished. Our system is already being crushed under the weight of the influx of illegal immigrants, which means we're unable to properly vet those coming in. We simply cannot safely be the sole or even primary destination of every immigrant or refugee. For this reason and for the many others outlined in this chapter, attempts at illegal immigration must be disincentivized and/or stopped.

As a Christian, I support accepting as many refugees and asylum seekers as we can thoroughly vet and approve. That number largely depends on the current capacity of our immigration system, which will always remain backlogged as long as our porous borders attract hundreds of thousands of illegal immigrants each year. I also support the legal immigration of people who will benefit their communities through their hard work, love of liberty, and responsibility.

There are good-faith immigration debates to be had among Christians, but the "we must allow everyone in per our Christian duty" isn't a serious position. Yes, we are exiles on this Earth, but we are not absolved of our responsibility to steward the places God has sovereignly put us.

In Jeremiah, God urges the Jewish exiles in Babylon to "seek the welfare of the city where I have sent you into exile, and pray to the Lord on its behalf, for in its welfare you will find your welfare" (Jer. 29:7). If Jews were supposed to seek the welfare of a nation that had conquered them, destroyed their people, and burned down Jerusalem, how much more should we Christian exiles steward our own nations today?

While compassion must be a part of the immigration conversation, we cannot allow one-sided empathy to guide our policy positions on such a far-reaching, complex issue. There must be thoughtful consideration of the importance of national sovereignty, the human need for order, and the practical needs of a nation.

Yes, Christians must care for the poor. Yes, we should desire to reach the lost. Yes, we should expend time, energy, and resources for persecuted Christians and impoverished people around the world. None of these things require us to support the unlimited acceptance of immigrants or the failure to secure our borders.

As good stewards, we must be agents of order. We must seek the good of our neighbors and nations, remembering that they, too, need our love, service, and evangelism.

Borders, military, and the existence of nation-specific laws and customs are still necessary to protect us from danger. This is the reality of a sin-stained world, but it will not always be this way. At the end of time, every nation, tribe, and people will stand before the throne of God together, singing the Lord's praises (Rev. 7:9). This passage highlights our earthly distinctions while pointing to an otherworldly unity made possible through Christ. Christians look forward to this future reality while recognizing we're not there yet, nor can we be, because such unity is impossible without Christ.

"Social Justice Is Justice"

Because the sentence against an evil deed is not executed speedily,
the heart of the children of man is fully set to do evil.

—ECCLESIASTES 8:11

ELIJAH McCLAIN WAS A YOUNG BLACK MAN, known for his love of music and animals. As a teen, he'd taught himself to play the guitar and the violin. He was homeschooled, and his mother allowed him to spend his lunch breaks playing music for the animals at the local animal shelter. His friends and family described him as a "peacemaker" who was "exceedingly gentle." He was also an "oddball," they said, and he had his quirks.

He liked to dance, by himself and in public. And sometimes he wore a ski mask, even when it was warm outside, due to a blood circulation disorder that made him feel cold. On the night of August 24, 2019, in his ski mask and warm clothes, Elijah was walking down the street in his hometown of Aurora, Colorado, and waving his arms, likely dancing to the music he loved so much.

A concerned onlooker called the police, reporting that a man wearing a ski mask and flailing his arms was walking down the street looking "sketchy." He noted that the man did not seem armed or dangerous. The police responded, confronting Elijah. According to police reports, Elijah got aggressive with the officers and reached for one of their guns, though the body-cam footage did not confirm this allegation.

Three officers pinned Elijah, who was five-foot-six and 140 pounds, to the ground. While restrained, he vomited between sobs. "I'm sorry. I wasn't trying to do that," he cried. "I can't breathe correctly." Paramedics on the scene injected Elijah with 500 milligrams of a sedative called ketamine, an amount well above the recommended dosage for a man his size. After he'd been handcuffed, one officer continued to restrain him with a carotid control hold, which rendered Elijah unconscious. He was taken to the hospital, where he died three days later. Neither the officers nor the paramedic involved in the incident were initially charged.

It was only after George Floyd's death that Elijah's story gained traction nationally. Demonstrations were held on his behalf, and a petition demanding further investigation into his case garnered over 5 million signatures. In response to the public outcry, in June 2020, Colorado governor Jared Polis and his administration opened a new investigation into the case. That same month, a troubling photo was published online, showing three officers standing across the street from a vigil for Elijah, one smiling officer seemingly mocking his death by pretending to put another officer in a choke hold.[1]

An investigative report released in February 2021 found that officers did not have a legal basis to stop or restrain Elijah. In October 2023, one of the three officers involved was found guilty of criminally negligent homicide and assault, and the two paramedics who administered the ketamine were found guilty of negligent homicide in December 2023.

Elijah's life was unnecessarily and unjustly taken by the very people who exist to protect us, and he's not the only one. Every year civilians are the victims of undue force by police officers, and the media insists this brutality disproportionately affects black people. Since

America's history is riddled with racial discrimination, it isn't hard to believe. And because many of the people who make this assertion are black, it's hard to disagree, particularly if you are white. Empathy leads us to affirm their pain, and the natural inclination is to then agree with the arguments presented and echo calls for systemic change to fix the problem of racial discrimination in policing.

But, as always, the truth is much more complicated than the popular narrative would suggest.

The Social Justice Hypothesis

Since 2020, the pervasive response to tragedies like Elijah's has been a call for social justice. Every American institution, we're told, is infested with racism, transphobia, and sexism. The only empathetic solution is to destroy the system.

Let's call this idea the social justice hypothesis. Its proponents argue that our inherently oppressive system costs the lives of innocent people at the hands of those in power. On social media and in the news, we read that people who identify as transgender are disproportionately more likely to be victims of violent crimes, that lesbian and gay people continue to face widespread discrimination, and that immigrants face systemic prejudice. Everyone but the straight, white male faces some sort of oppression that must be rectified.

Before we can decide whether the claims of the social justice hypothesis are true, let's define social justice. The United Nations defines it this way: "The fair and compassionate distribution of the fruits of economic growth."[2] This includes not just ensuring job opportunities, but combating everything that may affect one's ability to prosper: sexism, racism, transphobia, and other forms of discrimination. Social justice, in other words, is presented as the antidote to the large-scale bullying that keeps everyone but the white, straight male down.

Isn't this the moral, empathetic approach? Shouldn't we want people of all types to find success and safety? Isn't it right to oppose mistreatment of people on the basis of their skin color or gender? Shouldn't we want to build a world in which Elijah and others like him are treated equally and justly, in which a black man can listen to music and go on a walk without fearing for his life?

The answer to these questions may seem simple, especially to us Christians who are called to "seek justice" and "love mercy" (Mic. 6:8) and who worship a God who pays special attention to the marginalized and oppressed (Ps. 9:9, 146:7). Elijah's story reads like a case of deadly bullying in which the strong crushed the weak. And, even worse, these officers used not only their physical superiority but the power of the state to punish an innocent, defenseless man.

This is why so many Christians have accepted the social justice hypothesis: it promises to fight for the underdog and defeat the bully. After George Floyd's death in 2020, social justice felt more needed than ever, as we watched another helpless man call for his mother while being subdued by the police. Activists, journalists, influencers, and everyday people called for the dismantling of the racist systems that were said to have caused Floyd's killing.

Some Christian leaders lodged accusations of racism at those who rejected the social justice hypothesis. Beth Moore once told an audience: "To many in majority culture, and certainly in church culture, there is a very acceptable, sophisticated amount of racism. . . . White supremacy is so deeply ingrained in much of our white culture that if we haven't done the hard work to uproot it, it's highly unlikely we don't produce the fruit of it."[3] Pastor Eric Mason in Philadelphia went so far as to say "evangelicalism is anti-black" because white people believe that the effect of sin "applies to other people, but not to them."[4]

This occurred against the backdrop of the yearslong "racial reconciliation" movement within evangelicalism. While there may be various definitions of the term, the phrase most commonly means the effort of black and white Christians to find unity after years of disunity. While gospel-inspired unity is absolutely biblical, many components of the "racial reconciliation" discussed within the church are not.

Several popular books within evangelicalism, such as *Be the Bridge*, *White Awake*, and *The Color of Compromise* promote the necessity of so-called racial reconciliation. There may be important perspectives to be gleaned in each of these books, but they all include assumptions of the social justice hypothesis, asserting that white people today bear collective guilt and responsibility for the racial injustices of the past.

But "reconciliation" means to restore, or to bring back together. It denotes a previous relationship that has been broken. Is that the case between all white and black Christians? Only if one assumes the social justice hypothesis, which categorizes whole groups of people as oppressed or oppressors. But in reality, it's not accurate to say an entire group of people with one level of melanin have all wronged another group of people with another level of melanin. This is a secular, social justice idea, not a biblical one. Understanding the plight and position of someone who has a different background than you—having empathy for them—is one thing, and can be good. Forcing one group to bear responsibility for sins they did not themselves commit in the name of "reconciliation" is a form of toxic empathy bullying that is neither healthy nor godly.

This is where things get sticky: when social justice advocates move from righting wrongs to placing blame on groups of people they deem "oppressors" based not on individual actions, but on the group's identity, we get into dangerous territory, both politically and theologically. If social justice were simply the push to prevent future tragedies like Elijah's from happening, there would be little pushback. No one, and certainly not Christians who know Elijah's worth as an image bearer of God, wants more innocent lives taken by the police. No Christian wants to live in a world in which people are mistreated because of the color of their skin, their gender, or their socioeconomic status.

But those who push the social justice hypothesis aren't simply pointing out instances of injustice and offering solutions to prevent them in the future. Social justice is an inherently collectivist, power-seeking ideology. It seeks widespread, top-down, systemic change by forcefully shifting power (or perceived power) from one group to another. It encompasses other forms of _____ justice: economic justice, racial justice, reproductive justice, and so on. Social justice ideology can accurately be described as the mobilization of particular grievances to accomplish left-wing political goals.

These goals may be, in some cases, well intentioned, but good intentions are never enough. The questions we must ask of social justice advocates are: Are their claims true? Are their goals just? Are the outcomes of their policies and proposals helpful or harmful?

Let's look at social justice in action.

Social Justice Kills

The resounding call to empathy after George Floyd's and Elijah McClain's deaths demanded the defunding of—and even the abolition of—the police. Among Black Lives Matter's list of demands is the "national defunding of police" to save black people from deadly white supremacy.[5] In *The New York Times*, in an article titled "Yes, We Mean Literally Abolish the Police," Mariame Kaba states bluntly, "We can't reform the police," because policing still basically functions in its original form, as a slave patrol.[6] It wasn't enough to hold individual officers accountable. Rather, all cops were viewed as a part of the oppressor class, and activists insisted that "there are no good cops in a racist system."

Less radical activists argued for diminishing the number of police officers and minimizing their ability to arrest suspects. But both those who advocated for total abolition and for partial defunding shared the same belief: police are the problem. To them, these weren't just unfortunate incidents that demanded punishment for the officers and potential reforms within particular police departments. These were confirmations of their belief that, as a whole, policing in the United States is racist and must be torn down.

This was the goal of social justice in the summer of 2020: radical change of the criminal justice system to eliminate what they argued was the purposeful targeting of black people by the police, as well as prosecutors and judges.

Several of America's largest cities reduced or pledged to reduce police budgets in 2020. According to progressive organization Barnard Center for Research on Women, "Organizers successfully pushed for $840 million in police spending cuts. . . . Cities cut another $35 million by canceling contracts with police departments to patrol schools."[7] New York, Seattle, Los Angeles, Minneapolis, and other major cities all siphoned away millions of dollars from their police departments,[8] despite only 16 percent of Americans supporting the move.[9]

Did these revolutionary, top-down changes make communities more just?

The latest data shows that these communities were far *worse* off after the social justice agenda was enacted. Just a year later, cities were forced to reverse these budget cuts due to a sharp increase in murder.[10] Murder rates increased by double digits in many cities. At the end of 2020, homicides rose 32.2 percent in cities with a population of one million or more. In Baltimore, where the city council had cut $22 million from the police budget in 2020, city officials proposed a $27 million increase in 2021.

Given this trend, can we really accept the idea that social justice activism is the empathetic approach if the result is unmistakably violent? While not all social justice activists advocated for this kind of drastic policy change, few social justice activists openly opposed it, and many helped bring it to fruition by supporting organizations like Black Lives Matter. There is no evidence that such moves prevented cases like George Floyd's or Elijah McClain's, but there's ample evidence that they enabled the loss of innocent lives.

Defunding the police wasn't the only policy prescription offered by progressive activists at the time. They also pushed for more soft-on-crime policies throughout the justice system to eliminate the disparities between white and black people when it comes to arrests, prosecutions, and incarceration. District attorneys in America's largest cities, many of whom are funded by left-wing billionaire George Soros, refuse to prosecute many crimes. Progressive judges issue light sentences, allowing violent criminals to target more victims.

Thanks to progressive soft-on-crime policies, the U.S. saw a 24 percent decline in arrests along with a 30 percent increase in homicides in 2020—the highest spike ever recorded. Philadelphia had more homicides in 2020 than since 1990, and more killing than cities vastly larger, like New York or Los Angeles. This victimization disproportionately impacts black and Hispanic residents who live in high-crime areas.

In Los Angeles, the left-wing district attorney decided to stop prosecuting trespassing, disturbing the peace, driving without a license or with a suspended license, making criminal threats, drug use, public intoxication, possession of drug paraphernalia, loitering to commit prostitution, and resisting arrest. By downgrading these offenses from felonies to misdemeanors, California as a whole has effectively decriminalized stealing merchandize worth $950 or less, meaning criminals often just walk into a store and steal hundreds of dollars of items without ever being confronted by clerks, security, or law enforcement.

On two different occasions in 2021, Joseph Williams was arrested for domestic abuse, but San Francisco district attorney Chesa Boudin refused to bring charges against him.[11] Later that year, Williams murdered a seven-month-old baby. Steven Hutcherson had been arrested and released seventeen times before stabbing two teens in Grand Central Station in New York City in 2023.[12] According to police reports, he screamed "I want all the white people dead" before attempting murder. In 2021, Darrell Brooks drove his car into a Christmas parade in Waukesha, Wisconsin, killing six people, including an eight-year-old boy. Only weeks earlier, his girlfriend had accused him of running her over with the same car. Brooks's violent felony record dates back to 1999.[13]

Social justice activists also push for radical changes like the abolition of cash bail. According to data released by New York City officials, after the city prohibited judges from imposing monetary bail against most charges in 2020, "28% of those freed on supervised release were re-arrested on felony charges" and 50 percent were rearrested on misdemeanor charges within the year.[14]

In response to George Floyd's death, rioters burned down segments of Minneapolis. CNN infamously described the post–Jacob Blake riots as "fiery, but mostly peaceful," as Kenosha burned.[15] A woman burned down the Wendy's where Rayshard Brooks was shot. This was all motivated by the belief that the police are hunting down black people because of their skin color. Every effort to affirm that belief, negating the other mitigating facts, helped fan the flames—

both literally and figuratively. Innocent people's lives were lost or ruined in cities populated largely by black people. And yet, anyone pointing this out was met with the mallet of empathy that insisted compassion be felt only for the victims of allegedly racist police violence.

These social justice initiatives supported by organizations like Black Lives Matter created *more* black victims, not fewer. These victims are in addition to the black people killed in the BLM riots after George Floyd's death, like David Dorn in St. Louis, Antonio Mays, Jr., in Seattle, and eight-year-old Secoriea Turner in Atlanta. Meanwhile, tragic incidents like Elijah's may still occur.

While these efforts may decrease police interactions and the number of black people in jail, they also unnecessarily victimize innocent people. That's because social justice isn't real justice. It focuses on outcomes, like the number of black people in jail, rather than the "why" behind these numbers, and attempts to change those outcomes through policies that favor criminals.

Toxic empathy demands we ignore anyone hurt by a crime except the black suspect. But the result is more violence, not less.

Once we see the rotten fruits of social justice, it no longer looks like the empathetic option.

Social justice activists use stories like Elijah's to weaponize empathy in the advancement of an agenda that not only fails to protect innocent lives like his, but actually endangers the very lives it purports to defend.

How? By promoting assumptions that are simply not true.

The Myth of Systemic Racism

The assumption in the tragic killing of Elijah McClain was that he was targeted for his race. As with George Floyd, online activists demand that when a black person dies in an interaction with police, racism must be assumed. This is, we hear, the empathetic approach. We must "listen and learn" to and from those in the black community who say that the police are racist and that radical change is necessary. To argue with facts, figures, or counterpoints is maligned as arrogant and unkind.

But the uncomfortable truth is: we just don't know.

Let's look at some facts.

It's true that black people are disproportionately represented in the justice system. Though they comprise about 14.4 percent of the general population, they made up nearly 40 percent of the prison population[16] and about 26 percent of all arrests in 2019.[17] They are more likely than any other ethnicity to be involved in traffic stops and to be accused of reckless driving. They are also said to be more likely to be killed by the police than their white counterparts.[18] But it's important to note that densely populated black communities are typically high in crime, and black men, while making up only 5 to 6 percent of the population, account for 40 percent of police officer killings.[19] No one is arguing that this justifies tragedies like Elijah's. The point is that the more crime there is in a community, the more police interactions there are, and the greater the chances there are of a fatal interaction with the police.

According to a much-maligned study by Harvard professor Roland Fryer, black people are no more likely to be shot by the police than white people.[20] Any disparity in killings is likely due to the fact that black Americans are more likely to have interactions with the police, due to living in high-crime areas.

There is also a misunderstanding about how often suspects are shot by the police. One study found that self-identified progressives believe that one thousand to ten thousand unarmed black men are shot by the police every year. Conservatives guessed that the number is between ten to one hundred. The real number is typically between eight and twenty-seven.[21]

In 2019, the number of unarmed black men shot by the police was twelve, according to *The Washington Post*'s police shooting database. In 2021, that number dropped to eleven.[22] It's also important to note that "unarmed" does not necessarily mean not dangerous. A suspect that violently resists arrest, for example, can pose a deadly threat to a police officer who then chooses to use fatal force to protect both himself and innocent bystanders. While we all agree that the number of unwarranted deaths—by a gun or not—at the hands of the police should be zero, it's important to get a sense of the scale of the problem.

It's also worth noting that, compared to the eight unarmed black people killed by police in 2021, seventy-three police officers were killed by criminals that same year, including twenty-four who died in unprovoked attacks. To draw that out, some have estimated that roughly ten out of every one hundred thousand police officers were killed in 2021, while roughly one out of every ten million unarmed black people are killed by the police. Altogether, according to Heather Mac Donald at the Manhattan Institute, a police officer is four hundred times more likely to be killed by a black suspect than an unarmed black person is to be killed by a police officer.[23]

When it comes to social justice, empathy is weaponized to drown out any factual dissent with accusations of racism. It was considered racist to bring up the fact that Floyd was saying "I can't breathe" before officers even touched him, likely due to the amount of fentanyl in his system. Jacob Blake was shot in the back by police officers and his family was visited by then vice presidential nominee Kamala Harris after the incident. It was racist to mention that Blake was reaching for a knife in his car before he was shot. Rayshard Brooks was killed by the police, not for simply driving under the influence, but for fighting the two officers who pulled him over, stealing one of their

Tasers, and then trying to shoot them. Bringing these facts to light was considered—you guessed it—racist.

It may be that these officers still made grave errors in these interactions, and if so, they should be held to account. But there were enough factors at play that racism as the cause of the police's actions was extremely unlikely. The media disagreed. *The Washington Post* joined several other media outlets in asserting that George Floyd's life and death were marred by systemic racism.[24] The organization Injustice Watch published an article arguing that the Jacob Blake shooting highlighted the existence of systemic racism.[25] CNN described Rayshard Brooks as a man "kept down by a racist legal system."[26]

Progressive activists have been quick to spread these claims. The near unanimous conclusion on X after the George Floyd incident was that Chauvin was a raging racist. In response to the police officer who shot Jacob Blake walking free, Black Lives Matter declared that "there is no safety or justice in America for Black people."[27] Regarding Rayshard Brooks, Shaun King falsely suggested the police shot him while he was sleeping.[28]

You probably saw similar posts on your own timeline, shared by your friends, family, favorite influencers, and trusted mentors. It was hard to make sense of it, and pretty scary to try, because rebutting accusations of racism was met with such intense empathy shaming. But as we'll see next, their claims all committed the same dangerous logical error. They believed that disparities always mean discrimination—a notion the eminent economist Thomas Sowell has roundly debunked.

The Myth of Cosmic Justice

Just as disparities between white and black Americans when it comes to policing don't automatically prove racism, neither do disparities in other areas. Black-white disparities in income, graduation rates, home ownership, and employment are routinely pointed to as evidence of systemic racism. Works like *The New York Times'* "The 1619 Project" and the Netflix documentary *13th* claim that past injustices are the sole or primary cause of disparities and discrimination borne by black Americans today. If that is true, then, in the name of social justice, revolutionary change to how America functions is necessary.

Thomas Sowell, a black man who was born in the segregated South, has spent decades refuting this argument by pointing out that many gaps between white and black Americans grew exponentially *after* 1965, which marked the inception of Lyndon B. Johnson's welfare state. If slavery and Jim Crow were really the cause of today's outcomes for black America, these gaps would have been much wider sixty years ago than they are today, and yet they're wider today than they've ever been.[29]

It's certainly not hard to imagine that the well-documented historic prejudice toward black people in America could have a negative impact on them today, but this causal relationship must be proven rather than assumed. In *Discrimination and Disparities*, Sowell demonstrates that it is inaccurate and dangerous to "automatically and incessantly attribute statistical differences in outcomes to malevolent actions." The social justice–powered assumption that all disparities between white and black people are due to injustice leads to deleterious policies, like reducing a community's police force or doling out different sentences based on race.

Social justice ideology aims to eliminate all gaps between groups, operating on the belief that a just society is one in which all people obtain equal outcomes, what progressive ideologues typically refer to as "equity." Traditionally and biblically, "equity" refers to equal treatment. But, as Vice President Kamala Harris put it, equity, according to social justice, "means we all end up in the same place."

In *The Quest for Cosmic Justice*, Sowell argues that the attempt to force society to reach an unreachable, cosmic goal of complete equality of outcome is better named "cosmic" justice than social justice, since politicians and activists attempt to put themselves in the place of gods by rearranging society to achieve their vision of "equity." Sowell argues, "Envy was once considered to be one of the seven deadly sins before it became one of the most admired virtues under its new name, 'social justice.'"

Never before in history, he points out, has equality of outcome been achieved outside of the brute force of tyranny (think: communism). Differing outcomes among individuals and groups are expected, and while some disparities may be due to unjust discrimination, many are not. Choices, strengths and weaknesses, cultural differences, and many other factors can all play a part in a person's or community's outcomes. After all, if two siblings from the same family, who received the same upbringing, the same amount of parental support, and the same number of resources, can end up with vastly different outcomes, why would we expect people who come from varying backgrounds to all reach the same place?

Past discrimination or not, gaps in outcome are natural. Where these disparities can be proven to be caused by injustice, political remedies may be appropriate. But such calculations are exceedingly difficult to make, because, the truth is, all kinds of people have experienced past oppression.

Atrocities like slavery and Jim Crow laws are not unique to black people or the United States. Throughout world history, people of all nationalities and ethnicities have oppressed and have been oppressed, enslaving and being enslaved. Sowell highlights this often missed truth: "The very word 'slave' derived from the word for Slavs, who were enslaved by fellow Europeans for centuries before Africans began to be brought in chains to the Western Hemisphere." Africans were not enslaved by Westerners because of their skin color, but because, like all other slaves throughout history, they were available and vulnerable. Sowell goes on, "Slave-raiding continued in Africa, primarily by Africans enslaving other Africans and then, in West Africa, selling some of their slaves to whites to take to the Western Hemisphere."

This flies in the face of the social justice rendering of world and American history, which asserts that white people are concretely on the side of the oppressor, while black and brown people of the world are squarely on the side of the oppressed. It is against this oppressor-oppressed backdrop that social justice advocates conclude all disparities are proof of injustice.

Another point to consider: If disparities between white and black Americans are automatically due to racism in America, what about disparities between Asian and white Americans? Interestingly, in a supposedly white supremacist country, white people aren't supreme. When it comes to categories of success like education[30] and income,[31] Asian Americans take the cake. No one seriously believes Asian Americans have achieved more in these areas than white people because Asians are oppressing whites, so why should we assume disparities between white and black people are because of oppression?

Sowell explains, "The crucial question is not whether evils exist but whether the evils of the past or present are automatically the cause of major economic, educational and other social disparities today. The bedrock assumption underlying many political or ideological crusades is that socioeconomic disparities are automatically somebody's fault, so that our choices are either to blame society or to 'blame the victim.'" To social justice ideologues, there is no middle ground.

Dr. Voddie Baucham, a pastor, missionary, and dean of the School of Divinity at African Christian University in Zambia, described the problem with this reasoning as the "fallacy of the excluded middle." By attributing every disparate statistic to discrimination, social justice warriors are ignoring all the other factors that could come into play. These arguments lead to the justification of policies that purport to eliminate disparities in an effort to fight injustice.

Henry Rogers, who now goes by Ibram X. Kendi, rose to prominence in the summer of 2020 as the author of the book *How to Be an Antiracist*, which argued that discrimination against white people is the antidote to the mistreatment of black people: "The only remedy to racist discrimination is antiracist discrimination. The only remedy to past discrimination is present discrimination. The only remedy to present discrimination is future discrimination."

This principle has not only been applied to the justice system, but also in college admissions and employment. In 2023, the Supreme Court found that Harvard and other universities favored black and Hispanic applicants over better-qualified Asian and white applicants, violating the Equal Protection Clause of the Fourteenth Amendment.

According to Bloomberg, between 2020 and 2021, corporations who promised to hire more ethnic minorities followed through on their promise. Of the more than three hundred thousand jobs added by the S&P 100, only 6 percent were given to white candidates, despite white people constituting 60 percent of the U.S. population, meaning that a significant portion of white candidates were turned down because of their skin color.[32]

Just as discriminating against black people because of their skin color is wrong, so is discriminating against white people because of their skin color. Present discrimination doesn't actually rectify any past injustices, it just creates new ones.

This is the problem with the push for racial reparations as well. While social justice activists claim that the government must take money from white people and give it to black people to rectify the disparities caused by slavery and Jim Crow, even if this were an effective strategy in uplifting black America, stealing money from one racial group to give to another racial group is immoral. For all the talk of "ancestors" when it comes to reparations, we have little idea which white people today are related to slaveowners of the past, or which black people have enslaved predecessors. Are all white people really on the hook for something a small percentage of people who shared their skin color did two hundred years ago? Does a white poor person in Appalachia really owe money to Beyoncé and Barack Obama? Such is the absurdity of the demand for slavery reparations in America today.

This is what I mean when I say that social justice isn't justice: justice is about a fair and impartial *process*, whereas social justice is about equal *outcomes*. Lady Justice is blind, holding equal weights, but Lady Social Justice would have open eyes, assessing the skin color, socioeconomic status, sexual orientation, and other characteristics of each party and placing her thumb on the scales accordingly, in an attempt to rectify either real or perceived, past or present injustices against one party.

Social justice is only concerned with completely equal outcomes and will harness the power of the government to try to hold one group back while pushing another group forward. True justice, however, is concerned with equal treatment and fair processes, not equal outcomes.

God's Justice > Social Justice

The German philosopher Karl Marx mobilized the masses with the idea that the world is divided into two classes: the rich, oppressive bourgeoisie and the poor and downtrodden proletariat. The bourgeoisie was guilty as a whole, and the proletariat was virtually guiltless.

This idea has taken on many forms over the centuries, always resulting in chaos and death.

Take Robert Mugabe and Zimbabwe, for example. In the early 2000s, President Mugabe, a socialist, followed through on his promise to take land owned by white people and give it back to the black majority[33] in an effort to redress colonial-era land grabs.[34] This was accomplished through violence, terrorism, and the murder of white farmers, urging black Zimbabweans to "strike fear in the hearts of the white man, our real enemy."

Mugabe was a left-wing, social justice ideologue, a champion of the "black liberation struggle," who had imbibed the Marxist idea that people can be placed in oppressed or oppressor buckets based on a characteristic like skin color. Thus, present discrimination against the alleged oppressor, he thought, was necessary to rectify past discrimination against the supposed oppressed.

In doing so, he robbed Zimbabwe of its wealth. Once known as the breadbasket of Africa, the nation spiraled into squalor without the white commercial farmers. As it turns out, the black Zimbabweans who violently forced the white farmers off their land didn't possess the skills to farm commercially. While driving Zimbabwe into economic despair, Mugabe did what all socialists do: accumulated wealth for himself while his subjects starved. Though efforts have been made by Zimbabwe's new leadership to restore farms to their white owners, the nation still has not recovered from Zimbabwe's revolution.

Social justice is not justice. That's not only because it harms those it pretends to help, and it's not only because it's supported by philosophical and statistical errors.

It's not justice because it's *evil*. It is the opposite of what God calls justice.

Proverbs 20:10 tells us, "Unequal weights and unequal measures are both alike an abomination to the Lord." In God's law giving to ancient Israel, He prohibits favoritism, even to the poor: "You shall do no injustice in court. You shall not be partial to the poor or defer to the great, but in righteousness shall you judge your neighbor" (Lev. 19:15). Showing partiality is a perversion of justice that God disdains (Deut. 16:19; Prov. 24:23). God Himself shows no partiality, and we are to follow His example (Rom. 2:11; Gal. 2:6; Eph. 6:9; Col. 3:25; 1 Tim. 5:21; James 2:1, 9).

Just as mistreating someone because they're black is wicked, so is mistreating someone because they're white or because they're deemed "privileged." God doesn't see one form of mistreatment as less abominable than the other.

According to Scripture, God's justice has at least four characteristics: it is truthful, proportionate, impartial, and direct. We see this most clearly in God's lawgiving to ancient Israel.

Justice must be truthful: He prohibits spreading "a false report" or even abetting a lying witness (Ex. 23:1; Deut. 19:15–20). He forbids showing favoritism either to the poor or to the mighty (Ex. 23:3; Lev. 19:15). He demands proportionality—that the punishment fits the crime (Deut. 19:21). God's justice is also direct: while the consequences of a parents' sins may affect subsequent generations, children and grandchildren do not bear the guilt of their forefathers (Ex. 20:5. Ezek. 18:20).

All this means we don't judge people through the lens of intersectionality—by their wealth, status, skin color, or anything else. When it comes to the law, what matters is what someone actually *did*. And contrary to the demands to defund the police, God emphasizes the need for law enforcement in Romans 13, calling the government "an avenger who carries out wrath on the wrongdoer" (Rom. 13:4).

A fairly enforced law and an impartial justice system was God's idea, and He came up with it for our good. Not only does such a system bring order to society and protect the defenseless from harm, it also guarantees rights for the accused. In ancient Israel, those who were accused of a crime—man or woman, rich or poor—were afforded the right to a trial with trustworthy witnesses. This is how much God cared about His people and honored their innate dignity as image bearers of God.

This speaks to two parts of God's justice, referred to over two hundred times in the Old Testament as the Hebrew word *mishpat*. It means the equal, just application of laws and doling out just punishments. But it is not only about crime and punishment; it also means to give people their due, to recognize their worth as human beings, to show compassion and meet their needs.

God's heart for the poor, the fatherless, the widow, and other vulnerable members of society is made clear throughout Scripture, and our own words and actions should reflect that. The early church gives us an example of the kind of radical generosity to which Christians are called: "And they were selling their possessions and belongings and distributing the proceeds to all, as any had need" (Acts 2:45).

While social justice advocates may point to this verse to try to make their case for socialist policies, there's no support here for their arguments. These Christians gave their resources voluntarily, convicted by the Holy Spirit to do so. Social justice activists push for the *forced* forfeiture of resources, compelled by the government, in an effort to guarantee equal outcomes.

But the Lord loves a cheerful, willing giver, and He doesn't outline any expectation that giving, whether voluntarily or through our taxes, must aim to eliminate all disparities (2 Cor. 9:7). God hates

injustice, and we should, too, but opposing injustice may not eliminate disparities, and eliminating disparities certainly will not end injustice.

The draw of social justice remains strong, however. Our natural
and good tendency to feel empathy for the underdog makes the oppressed versus oppressor narrative attractive and its promises to uplift
the marginalized appealing.

Christians, in particular, want to help those on the lowest rungs
of society. In following the example of Christ, we are obligated to do
so. But if we're not careful, our righteous compassion for the poor
can be exploited to support the policies that hurt the very people
we're trying to help.

The problem is that so-called Christian social justice is completely
at odds with God's justice. Take Latasha Morrison's idea of racial
reconciliation, for example, from *Be the Bridge*. Reconciliation implies
that one group has wronged the other. But it cannot be accurately
said that white people as a whole have harmed black people as a whole.
This is an oppressor-oppressed dynamic that we find in secular social
justice ideology, not in the Bible.

Here's another example. Morrison uses the biblical accounts of
Ezra and Daniel to try to demonstrate communal responsibility for a
nation's sins. She notes that these men were "personally innocent . . .
but they came under guilt and shame nonetheless." Carrying the
weight of guilt and shame over slavery and discrimination, she argues,
is a necessary part of "true reconciliation and justice."

But Morrison seems to miss key distinctions between these stories
and the responsibility of white Americans today. Ezra and Daniel
were a part of a covenant people, Israel, who were still engaging in the
sins of which Ezra and Daniel were asking for forgiveness (Ezra 9:7).
Neither white people nor white evangelicals are part of a distinct,
covenant group. It makes no sense, logically or biblically, to hold

these roughly defined groups responsible for the past sins of people who generally looked like them and lived in the same relative vicinity. She seemingly ignores that the Bible forbids forcing a person to pay for their ancestors' sins (Ezek. 18:20).

And yet this is Morrison's entire foundation for her definition of racial reconciliation, which she argues requires white people to pay reparations in the form of "yielding influence, decentering [y]our own experience, letting go of privilege." "Bridge builders," she says, "must return what was taken, even if it hurts." This seems to me a push for division rather than unity.

Such divisiveness is evidenced in the guidelines for Be the Bridge groups. In a public document once titled "Whiteness 101," white participants in Be the Bridge are held to a totally different standard than black participants. They are forbidden from "whitesplaining" by explaining away a "microaggression" a black person has experienced. They must maintain "a posture of active listening." If a black participant expresses offense at their words, they shouldn't justify themselves but rather must "apologize and do better next time." They must make space for black people to "wail, cuss, or even yell" at them without getting upset. Any expression of frustration or offense is "white fragility" showing up.

Does this sound like the Christlike path to gospel unity? It doesn't, because it's not.

This is not to say that black and white Christians don't need to better understand one another. We can acknowledge some uncomfortable truths: White Christians, as the majority, may indeed have to work harder to see the point of view of their black brothers and sisters in Christ, and to empathize with any ethnicity-specific struggle they may have had. It's true that white and black people can have different life experiences because of their race, and it's good to understand these varying backgrounds. But placing blame on one group because of their melanin levels, while alleviating responsibility of another group because of their melanin levels, is not only unbiblical; history shows us it's a recipe for disaster.

Within evangelicalism, conversations about social justice, especially as it pertains to race, have taken center stage. This has caused much division within the church in a way that almost no other issue has. In my view, social justice is the most deceiving and pervasive form of empathy weaponization, and it has a special hold on many Christians that is much stronger than that of abortion or transgenderism. There are threads of biblical truth woven into the social justice narrative that evoke Christians' empathy, and therefore it is the one form of progressivism that is not only accepted within conservative evangelicalism, but promoted. Christians who embrace the tenets of social justice, especially when it comes to race, are continually hoisted up as trustworthy biblical expositors.

There are other manifestations of social justice ideology within evangelicalism, including opposition to the death penalty. While not all Christians who oppose the death penalty are social justice advocates, they are usually motivated by the shared belief that that form of punishment is unjust.

I don't want to minimize the fact that there are many thoughtful, solid believers who hold this position and will offer theological support for their views, but I do see this as another product of empathy-manipulation. The truth is there is no basis in Scripture for the belief that the death penalty is categorically unjust.

In Genesis 9:6 God told Noah, "Whoever sheds the blood of a man, by man shall his blood be shed, for God made man in his own image." It is because man is so uniquely valuable, and because God loves people so much, that He declares execution the only just punishment for murder. Intentionally killing an innocent person is *that* big of a deal to Him. God's command to Noah predates Israel and is backed by a reasoning still true today: man is made in God's image. This is not just an Old Testament rule, as we can see in Romans 13:1-4, but a principle we'd be wise to apply today.

Justice—how we define it, how it's carried out—matters immensely, because people matter immensely. It is no small task to decide how to enforce laws when law enforcement (or the lack thereof) affects so many individuals, families, and communities. Christians don't always have to agree on every law or every verdict, but we should be united in studying God's Word and seeking His will in all things, including how we order our nation. Remember: laws and governments were God's ideas and they are supposed to exist for our good. Ideally, they keep evil in check and protect us from the harm and chaos caused by unfettered wickedness. It's our job, as agents of God's order, to do what we can to ensure our laws align with God's basic principles of justice He outlines in Scripture. This does not mean Christians are pushing for a theocracy, as we don't see that example set for us in the New Testament, but it does mean, like everyone else in American life, we unapologetically allow our worldview, informed by the Great Lawgiver, to drive our policy positions. It is God's justice, not toxic empathy-laden social justice, that must be our guide.

Conclusion

IN THE BEGINNING, THERE WAS DARKNESS. There was no form, no noise, no shadow or shades of color. The earth was empty. But God was there, as He'd always been, His Spirit hovering over the waters. He was up to something—something new. At once, He spoke, His voice piercing through the void and demanding light. And the light was good. The good light was called "Day," and the darkness called "Night." So time began, every moment ticking at the behest of its Creator.

Then God spoke the rest of the universe into being. The land and the plants, the seas and the stars, the birds and the beasts. Teeming with sights and sounds, the universe echoed with praise of God's creativity and goodness. And yet His work wasn't yet complete. On day six of His creation, God made a being unlike anything else He'd called into existence, a being made in His own image: man. This man was given dominion over the earth, charged with cultivating the garden, naming the animals, and keeping all that God had made. But it was not good for the man to be alone. Thus God made him a helper called "woman." So the first man and woman, Adam and Eve, were made, bestowed with the responsibility of filling and caring for the world.

Adam and Eve's universe was filled with harmony, peace, unlimited sustenance, unhindered beauty, and uninhibited relationship with the Creator of all things. It's hard for us to imagine even a moment without worry, yet their days were filled only with calm. That nagging suspicion that something's not right, the unrelenting feeling that things aren't as they should be, the constant concern about one thing or another, the fear of what's to come, the dreadful realization that one day we and everyone we love will die . . . these emotions and experiences we call "human" were totally foreign to them. They knew only happiness.

All God had created was theirs to enjoy, with one exception. In the center of the Garden of Eden stood the Tree of the Knowledge of Good and Evil. The fruit from this tree, God told them, they must not eat, or else they will die. With the rest of the world at their fingertips, surely this would be an easy command to obey.

But the craftiest creature in the Garden, the serpent, had it out for Adam and Eve, and he seduced Eve with a simple question: "Did God actually say, 'You shall not eat of any tree in the garden'?" That's not what God had said, and Eve told him so. She corrected the snake: "God said, 'You shall not eat of the fruit of the tree that is in the midst of the garden, neither shall you touch it, lest you die.'" The serpent assured Eve no such tragedy would occur. She would simply "be like God," understanding the difference between good and evil. So Eve ate, then Adam, and mankind fell. We fell into sin and out of a perfect relationship with God, into suffering and out of the bliss of Eden.

The rest is history—a bitter, bloody history. From Adam and Eve's disobedience sprung every bit of brokenness we see in this life: all manner of sin, sadness, sickness, death, and decay. Abortion, gender confusion, sexual immorality, lawlessness, and injustice are all consequences of the Fall. They're all symptoms of disorder, of the brokenness of a world that groans for redemption from its Creator (Rom. 8:22).

With only a question, Satan sent humanity into a spiral of destruction. "Did God actually say . . . ?" The Great Deceiver presented Eve with a half-truth. It was true God didn't say not to eat any fruit. It was also true that the fruit would open their eyes to the reality of good and evil, and Satan acknowledged that. But it was the consequence of their choice that Satan obscured: He denied the death behind the disobedience. He caused Eve to question God's trustworthiness and tempted her with power. "Do this, and 'you will be like God.'" For both Adam and Eve, the temptation to replace God with the god of self was irresistible, so they ate, and we fell.

And we continue falling, seduced by the same question with which the devil tricked Eve. "Did God actually say . . . ?" All sin starts with doubt of God's goodness and the creeping suspicion that perhaps we know better than Him. Maybe He doesn't really know best. Maybe I do. When we disobey God's Word, we follow our feelings and insist on our own way—often, like Adam and Eve, when it hurts us.

So it is with toxic empathy, which tells us that we can be more loving and wiser than God by affirming sin.

"Did God actually say you shouldn't love the woman in crisis?"

"Did God actually say you shouldn't love transgender people?"

"Did God actually say you shouldn't love the gay person, the immigrant, or the criminal?"

No, God didn't. Christians are indeed called to love. But He does call us to truth and obedience, and He does tell us that real love can't exist without both. And His Word shows us that disobedience to God never ends well.

But, Satan may say: Isn't that legalistic? Isn't that pharisaical, overly religious, divisive, judgmental? Aren't you called to tolerance, acceptance, and empathy? How do you think that person feels? They're oppressed, marginalized, in pain. Wouldn't you like someone to affirm you and celebrate your choices? Surely the empathetic approach will win them over. You can worry about the rest later.

Just a little compromise. Just a slight softening of the truth. Just a slight departure from Scripture. Just a small dose of worldliness. It's kind. It's for the greater good. What will it hurt? "You will not surely die . . ."

Satan is crafty, but he's not creative. Through toxic empathy he's dishing out the same lie to women today that he hissed to Eve in the Garden. Many of us are falling for it.

Yes, toxic empathy is satanic. It is a tool of the Deceiver to convince women that biblical love means affirming someone's sin. It makes its victims weak-kneed and simpleminded, convincing them that standing up against evil is mean and that niceness is an acceptable replacement for obedience to God.

When God Is Right, He's Right

Christians are commanded to love, and empathy can help us love well. But empathy without biblical truth isn't love at all—it's hate. It's hate, because—just as Satan did with Eve in the Garden—affirming sin means nudging someone off the edge of the cliff. It means helping them toward the thing that's going to destroy them and those around them. It means both spiritual and physical harm, leading to temporal and eternal ramifications. Would you push someone you love off a cliff? Would you lead them toward destruction? Would you encourage them to do something that's going to cause them pain and death?

Yes, God does demand Christians love our neighbors. But He also prohibits murdering babies. He also made us male and female. He defined marriage as a union between a man and woman, He created borders and laws, and He hates injustice.

God is love, so everything He says and does is said and done in perfect love. So His commands and boundaries are in place because of His love for us, not despite it. They are for our good. He wants joy and peace and eternal life for us. He wants to bring order to our lives.

Because God is love, we cannot outlove him. The most loving thing will always be to agree with Him. So, if we love those around us, we will be vessels of His goodness and order. That means advocating for the life of an unborn child is loving. Recognizing the beauty of the male-female binary is loving. Honoring the sacred, life-giving definition of marriage is loving. Protecting a nation's sovereignty for the good of its citizens is loving. Punishing the wrongdoer for the sake of the innocent and weak is loving. The flip side of these things— murder, mutilation, perversion, lawlessness, and chaos—only yields disordered, harmful outcomes. God's ways are better; the most loving thing we can do is agree with them.

This isn't to say you'll be right about everything, or that your critics will never have a valid complaint. Some of these issues—like abortion, transgenderism, and marriage—are very clear-cut in the Bible. Others are much more debatable: the Bible certainly allows defined borders and punishing criminals, but Christians disagree in good faith on how government defines and enforces those laws. Nothing I'm saying here should be interpreted to mean that there are zero nuances to these subjects. Certainly our salvation does not depend upon what we think of, for example, border security or the death penalty, which is good news, since none of us knows the perfect set of policy prescriptions or one surefire solution. We should, however, be able to agree on what's a biblical principle and what's not, and work together with this unified understanding.

The point is, Lord knows I've needed the correction of fellow

Christians, and I always will. This is a part of every Christian's sanc-
tification. But when you know something is factually and/or biblically true, and you know you are doing everything you can to speak
the truth in love, your job is to stand firm. Don't bend the knee to the
bullies. Don't apologize for what you are not sorry for.

As Christians who are called to wisdom and reason, we simply can't
allow empathy to make us stupid, to obscure what's true in favor of
what feels good (Rom. 16:19; James 3:17). That leads us to speak, act,
and vote in a way that creates a society that makes it easy to celebrate
sin and difficult to champion virtue. Everyone eventually suffers.

One of our jobs as Christians is to mitigate human suffering, especially the suffering of the powerless. The history of the church is
marked by this kind of advocacy, and we're tasked with carrying this
baton today.

When Children Became People

Satan seems to have it out for children. They are always the most vulnerable prey to Satan's schemes. Mentally and physically less developed than adults, children don't have the tools to defend themselves
against the more powerful. They are easily moldable, for better and
for worse. Parents are to offer spiritual, mental, and physical protection to their children, while Satan and his cohorts will always seek
their spiritual, mental, and physical destruction.

This idea is captured in much of dystopian literature. In *Brave
New World*, babies are grown in "pods," have no natural family, are
desensitized to sex at an early age, and become brainwashed ambassa-
dors of "the system." In *1984*, children become enemies of their parents in defense of Big Brother.

Look throughout history, and the cultures most controlled by

Satan have been marked by the exploitation of children, forcing children into slavery and prostitution, offering them as sacrifices to gods, or using them to advance a political agenda. From ancient Carthage to the Aztecs to precolonial West Africa, babies and children were sacrificed to satisfy the demands of pagan deities. In ancient Rome, children were often used as sexual objects for powerful men. Throughout the twentieth century, children became foot soldiers of dictatorial regimes like Hitler's Germany and Pol Pot's Cambodia.

Today, we're not so different from our pagan predecessors. It's just that our bloodthirst has been given politically correct names, such as "abortion" and "gender-affirming care." We are still very much in the barbaric business of butchering children's bodies and exploiting them as political objects. One could even argue it's still a form of sacrifice to a kind of god. Some may say it's the gods of progressivism, or of social justice, or the god of empathy. I like to say that these are sacrifices made to the god of self, who is relentless and merciless in his demands for the satisfaction of his desires.

The god of self tells a woman her wants and needs are more important than the life of her child. The god of self tells a person that their feelings about their gender are more important than reality. The god of self tells adults that their sexual desire is more important than a child's need for a mother and father. The god of self even convinces us that lawlessness—either through open borders or social justice—is a sophisticated, compassionate position that will make us appear loving and righteous. Our age is ruled by self-deification.

Children, helpless and needy as they are, are always the first victims of the reign of the god of self. Children suffer most from abortion, gender deception, sexual depravity, and the chaos that accompanies a failure to enforce the law. Whether they're being murdered in the womb or trafficked at the border, children bear the brunt of disorder.

This isn't primarily a political statement. My argument is not that every Republican policy is good or every Democratic policy is evil. I am saying that, on these issues, the "progressive" position is the more destructive and disordered one, the one that carries far more danger to our nation in general and children in particular, the one that's placing children on the altar of the god of self, carrying on humanity's ugly history of sacrificing the young in service to the powerful.

But child sacrifice does not have to persist unfettered. In fact, we have a model for its abolition in the Christian church. In his book *When Children Became People*, O. M. Bakke offers a historical analysis of the treatment of and ideas surrounding children in ancient, pagan Greece and Rome, and how they were disrupted by the dawn of Christianity.

In looking at the writings of Plato, Aristotle, and others, Bakke highlights the consensus around the concept of *logos*, the Greek word for "word, reason, or speech." These philosophers believed that societies and nation-states are held together by logos, and the only kind of person that really possessed logos was the adult, free male. This set him apart from slaves, barbarians, the sick, the elderly, women, and children. Children were viewed on the same level as animals. They didn't possess logos, and therefore they were useless to the cohesion of a nation.

Children's mental and physical weaknesses were used as the pretext for their exploitation. Children in these societies, especially children from nonwealthy families, were neglected, abused, and sexually objectified. Abortion was a widespread practice. And if the child was born, because of the high childhood mortality rate, emotional and financial investment in them was often viewed as a waste.

At best, parents saw children as an investment in their future, as someone to take care of them in their old age, or, if possible, inherit their possessions. At worst, they were regarded as a drain on resources that could be used and abused as adults saw fit.

In these cultures, a person's value was measured by gender, status, and most of all, the capacity for rationality. The idea of innate worth was foreign to the leaders and scholars of this era, and certainly there was no concept of offering greater care to the weak and vulnerable.

What changed? How did those on the margins of society, and in particular, children, go from being regarded as objects to a specially protected class that we view as precious?

The answer is Christianity. Christianity changed everything. The same belief system that interrupted all the debauchery in the ancient Greek and Roman world—the gender bending, the rampant prostitution, the oppression of women and the elderly—also moved the sick and the disabled from the outskirts of society into hospitals, moved the homeless into homes, put food in the mouths of the hungry, and upheld children as dignified people deserving of care and protection.

The ancient writers of pagan Greece and Rome believed that a person's logos—their ability to rationalize—gave them worth.

And it took Logos, the Word made flesh, Jesus Christ, arriving as a baby, to abolish that dangerous idea.

"In the beginning was the Word (*logos*), and the Word was with God, and the Word was God. He was in the beginning with God. All things were made through him, and without him was not any thing made that was made. In him was life, and the life was the light of men. The light shines in the darkness, and the darkness has not overcome it" (John 1:1–5).

The logos of the Greeks and the Romans said "children have no value." The Logos of Christianity said "Let the little children come to me and do not hinder them, for to such belongs the kingdom of heaven" (Matt. 19:14)."

The heavenly Logos—the Word of God—the Word made flesh—trumped the worldly logos, making "foolish the wisdom of the world" (1 Cor. 1:20).

He introduced the radical concept of innate human worth that is rooted in our creation as image bearers of God, as we read in Genesis 1, and is further emphasized by the gospel, which, as Ephesians 2 tells us, means we are all equally dead in our sins apart from Christ, and by grace through faith can be made equally alive through Him.

Equal in worth. Equally in need of a Savior. Male or female, Jew or Greek, slave or free, brown or white, child or adult, disabled or able-bodied, rich or poor. Equal in worth, in equal need of a Savior.

This Jesus, who introduced the world to this radical message, who flipped the world upside down and turned what the world thought they knew on its head, specifically attended to those whom the pagan scholars of the time disdained and ignored.

He locked eyes with the bleeding woman, He touched the leper, He fed the hungry, He gave strength to the paralyzed, He regarded the poor, He forgave the prostitute, He dined with the tax collectors, upholding their value not just through His attention and help but by calling them all to faith and repentance.

Jesus Christ, His gospel, and the Christians He sent out changed everything, revolutionizing how the world saw people. He put to shame the academics and rulers of the time, who thought they had mastered the understanding of human nature and hierarchy and nation building.

It was this gospel that changed the ancient world, fueled the abolition of slavery in America, and remains the motivation for Christian efforts today in protecting the vulnerable from harm.

At her best, the church has stood as a refuge of clarity and courage in an age of chaos and confusion. We have stood in the gap for children, protecting them from the predation of the powerful. We are still called to do so today.

This is why Christians must wade into culture and politics. It is one way that we save children from slaughter and honor their dignity, just as our predecessors did.

Children are always the unconsenting subjects of progressive social experiments: from abortion, to the redefinition of the family, to reproductive technology, to gender ideology, to government policies that push their safety and well-being to the wayside.

The world would have you believe that Christians—particularly Christian conservatives—should separate our faith from our political engagement. They call our engagement "Christian nationalism" or "Christofascism" and insist that to really love our neighbor, we must vote against our conscience and biblical principles. But this is a trick of the devil. Every single person votes in accordance with their world-view, no matter what their belief system is. We, too, have both the right and the responsibility to do the same.

Every law is based on a moral belief. The only question is ever, "Which one?" Will it be Christianity, Islam, atheism, or something else? There's no neutrality, and there never has been.

America was founded upon the assumption that there is a Creator who has given us rights that the government doesn't have the power to arbitrarily take away (see: the Declaration of Independence). The founders, while they possessed various forms of belief in God, agreed that God's power transcended that of the government. They honored Him as the source of truth, morality, wisdom, rights, and innate human dignity. The charters of America's first states all included the necessity of the Christian faith for all elected officials. There was no question that Christianity was and must be the foundation for their revolutionary, free society to flourish.

America has been at her best when she has remembered that foundation. The abolition of slavery represented a nation hearkening back to her Christian roots that declared all people equal, and it was the gospel of Jesus Christ that led that charge.

So it must be today: Christians must always lead the charge on behalf of the most vulnerable by advocating for order and true justice. This doesn't always mean politics and culture wars, but often it does.

As you may have heard me say over the years: politics matter because policy matters because people matter. Politics affects policy and policy affects people, and people matter to God.

If we believe what we say we do about God, that he is the Creator of all things, then that necessarily affects how we engage in politics and culture. If He is the Creator of all of it, He is the Authority over all of it. He is the definer of truth and the arbiter of morality. He declares what is and what isn't, what's right and what's wrong, what's good and what's evil, what's true and what's false, what a woman is and when life begins. It is impossible to separate Genesis 1:1—"God created the heavens and the earth"—from the rest of life. It affects everything.

This truth should give us the utmost courage: that Jesus, who is the same yesterday, today, and forever, has given us the same power that he's given Christians throughout history to resist evil and be agents of order and goodness. Whether suffering under Nero or Newsom, Christ's followers can stand firm against the chaos of the world. We can rebuff the empathy shaming and bullying that would have us kowtow to the mobs. We can reject people pleasing and mainstream popularity and instead advocate for what is good, right, and true.

Expect Unfair Criticism

We can expect to face the same or worse criticism when we defend the unborn, contradict radical gender theory, support traditional marriage, or take a stand on any contentious issue. For speaking truth-filled love, you will be called names. You will be accused of hate and bigotry. Even people who call themselves Christians will chastise you for not being worldly enough. They may police your tone or tell you you're making a big deal out of things that don't matter.

Maybe you'll be called a Pharisee, or something silly like that. But remember: Jesus called out the Pharisees not because they cared too much about holiness but because they didn't care about it enough. They knew the law and followed it, but they didn't get that true obedience comes from the heart. They looked good, but inside they followed the god of self, not the God of Scripture.

Following the God of Scripture will always be controversial. Saying what He says will always be condemned, no matter how gentle or nice we are. Jesus, the perfect embodiment of love, was "full of grace and truth" (John 1:14). He was filled with compassion and a sincere desire to see lost people saved, which motivated Him to tell the truth.

There is another person in the Bible who is given a similar description: Stephen. He is described as being "full of grace and power" (Acts 6:8). Filled with the Holy Spirit, he stood in front of a crowd and told them of their sins and need for salvation.

Who wouldn't want to be described in the same way Jesus and Stephen were? Full of grace, power, and truth—consumed by love and the desire to share God's truth.

And yet what were their fates? Jesus was crucified, and Stephen was stoned to death. Despite being filled with grace, despite their kindness and gentleness, they ignited the ire of angry mobs, who delivered them unto death.

It's tempting as Christians to believe that we can be nicer than God, that we can appeal to people better by being more polite or gentler than He is. We feel like we need to take God off the hook for the harsher things He's revealed through Scripture. Maybe if we're squishy or silent or secular enough on the controversial issues of our day, then the world will like us. Then we'll have earned enough of their respect, we think, to be heard by them, so we can lead them to Christ.

But this is both unbiblical and ineffective. It's self-idolatry: believing we are more loving and wiser than God, who is the source of all wisdom and is love itself (James 1:5; 1 John 4:8). We will never out-strategize Him in appealing to the unbelieving world. People are won over by Christian courage, not Christian compromise. The Word of God never returns void (Isa. 55:11); we have no such promise about our own words.

Consider the story of Laura Perry Smalts, whose transformation we discussed in the chapter on gender. It was her parents' insistence on calling her by her name, referring to her by her true pronouns, and reminding her of God's words that the Holy Spirit used to change her. Recall Maria, the woman overwhelmed by the charity of pregnancy center volunteers, who chose life and followed Jesus because truth was shared with her: truth about the life in her womb and the gospel.

This is the result of choosing true love over toxic empathy.

One Day

Toxic empathy isn't just a cheap replacement for real, biblical love. It is its foil, its archnemesis. It's the wolf dressed as a grandmother to trick Red Riding Hood. It is the villain who poses as an innocent civilian so he can gain access to his victims. It's a poisonous dessert, sweet to taste but deadly when consumed.

Here's the good news, the best news of all: One day, toxic empathy won't exist. We won't have to worry about it, because there will be no one to manipulate us and nothing to be manipulated by. There will be no more debates, no more politics.

There will be no more abortion. Every murdered baby will be alive and whole.

There will be no more gender confusion or perversion. Every spiritual body will be exactly as God intends it to be.

There will be no more sexual immorality. Everyone will rejoice completely in God's good design and purposes. The only marriage celebrated will be the one between Christ and his church.

There will be no more migration, no asylum seeking or fleeing for refuge. There will be no more danger, or enemies, or economic needs. There will be one perfect city, the New Jerusalem, where all God's children are citizens of our new eternal home.

There will be no more injustice, murder, or oppression. There will only be peace, and perfect justice will rule once and for all.

All the wretched, bloody brokenness humanity has endured since Adam and Eve took that fateful bite of the forbidden fruit will come to an end. We will once again walk in unhindered communion with our Creator. Sorrow, sickness, and sin will be no more.

Because Jesus wins. At the end of this mess, Jesus comes in on a white horse and avenges innocent blood. He destroys the Enemy once and for all. The serpent's head will be crushed, and all God's children, all those who have been made alive in Christ by grace through faith, will live with Him in perfect joy forever.

So we can feel overwhelmed with the work we have ahead of us in our generation. We can agree that our country is in a scary place, maybe even a place beyond the point of no return. But the future outcome of our country isn't up to us. It's up to God, who will work things out according to His good providence, and who promises the Church ultimate victory in the end.

Our job is to simply do the next right thing, in faith, with excellence, and for the glory of God. At all times, in all places, that is all the Christian is called to do. That requires us to be brave, thoughtful, discerning, reasonable, hopeful, cheerful, grateful, and steadfast. It is to beautify and cultivate the tiny spot in the universe, the miniscule speck of eternity, in which God has purposely set us.

Sometimes this may mean public acts of courage. Perhaps God

gives you a platform to speak unpopular but much-needed truth. Perhaps he is putting you in a position of leadership to affect change in your community. Sometimes it means simply changing your baby's diaper with joy or cheerfully doing the task assigned to you by your boss. It is very often the latter: those unseen, unsung moments where we choose to honor God in thought, word, and deed.

No matter what this looks like, we cannot do God's work as cowards. Not all of us are called to have a public platform. Not everyone is called to be actively engaged in the political and cultural wars. But we all have a role in speaking truth to a world drowning in deceit, to be a refuge of clarity in a world thrown by chaos. And we are all called to care, in some capacity, about these problems our nation is facing, because they all affect people. Remember: politics matter because policy matters because people matter. Politics affect policy, and policy affects people, and people matter. We Christians, who see our neighbors as image bearers of their Creator, should understand that better than anyone.

And so we do what we can with what we're given, raising a respectful ruckus for the truth on behalf of our children and communities. We rebuff attempts at emotional manipulation hoisted upon us by toxic empathy and instead rely on God's Word and the capable minds he gave us as our guides. Over and over again, we choose truth-filled love over its poisonous counterpart, trusting that God's ways are better and more loving than any the world could muster.

Whatever work God calls you to do, I pray he gives you strength and good cheer. And know I'll be here, happily sharing the arrows. You're not alone. In our stand for truth and true love we are never alone, because God is always with us—and remember: in the end, He wins.

Acknowledgments

Many thanks are due! First to the Lord, who has never failed me—not even once. His faithfulness and kindness sustain me and make all of life worth living.

Thank you to my husband for loving me and our girls so well and for making all the good things in our lives possible.

Thank you, Mom and Dad: your daily encouragement and wisdom keep me grounded and build me up more than you know. Thanks to Helen Cunningham at Sentinel. You believe in me, breathe life into my ideas, and are so patient and flexible as I try to navigate book-writing amid the rest of life's demands. I'm grateful also to Bria Sanford, whose enthusiasm and support ensured this book got done and got done well.

This book wouldn't exist without Alec Torres, who understood my vision from the get-go and quickly and skillfully helped turn my streams of consciousness into *Toxic Empathy*.

To Maura Teitelbaum, my book agent: there's no one else I'd rather represent and help me in this ever-changing publishing world! Thank you for all of your hard work. To my *Relatable* community:

thank you for allowing my voice to be heard. Thank you for listening, watching, reading, and, most of all, for praying and encouraging through all of these years. Sharing the arrows with you always.

There are so many others who have indirectly contributed to the completion of this book by their involvement in various aspects of my life. I'm thankful for you all!

Notes

Introduction

1. Ellie Krasne, "Black Families Matter," Heritage Foundation, June 29, 2021, https://www.heritage.org/marriage-and-family/commentary/black-families-matter.
2. Yaron Steinbuch, "BLM Co-Founder Describes Herself as 'Trained Marxist,'" *New York Post*, June 25, 2020, https://nypost.com/2020/06/25/blm-co-founder-describes-herself-as-trained-marxist/.
3. Lois Beckett, "At Least 25 Americans Were Killed During Protests and Political Unrest in 2020," *The Guardian*, October 31, 2020, https://www.theguardian.com/world/2020/oct/31/americans-killed-protests-political-unrest-acled.
4. Kamala Harris, Twitter post, November 1, 2020, 1:06 P.M., @KamalaHarris, https://twitter.com/KamalaHarris/status/1322963321994289154?lang=en.

LIE #1: "Abortion Is Health Care"

1. Bob Hayton, "R.C. Sproul on Abortion," Fundamentally Reformed, January 21, 2011, https://www.fundamentallyreformed.com/2011/01/21/r-c-sproul-on-abortion/.
2. Testimony of Jill L. Stanek, R.N., United States House of Representatives Committee on the Judiciary, May 23, 2013, https://web.archive.org/web/20141207151142/https://judiciary.house.gov/_files/hearings/113th/05232013/Stanek%2005232013.pdf.
3. Centers for Disease Control and Prevention, "Mortality Records with Mention of Termination of Pregnancy," https://www.cdc.gov/nchs/health_policy/mortality-records-mentioning-termination-of-pregnancy.htm.
4. "Questions and Answers on Born-Alive Abortion Survivors," Charlotte Lozier Institute Fact Sheet, January 27, 2023, https://lozierinstitute.org/questions-and-answers-on-born-alive-abortion-survivors/.
5. "Doctor Investigated in Badly Botched Abortion," NBC News, February 5, 2009, https://www.nbcnews.com/id/wbna29037216#.UZyw3YKOf9I.
6. In the Court of Common Pleas, First Judicial District Of Pennsylvania, Criminal

Trial Division, In Re: Misc. No. 0009901-2008, County Investigating: Grand Jury XXIII, Report of the Grand Jury, January 14, 2011, https://cdn.cnsnews .com/documents/Gosnell,%20Grand%20Jury%20Report.pdf.

7. Steven Ertelt, "Late-Term Abortion Doc Caught Comparing Unborn Baby to Meat in a Crock-Pot," LifeNews, May 8, 2013, https://www.lifenews.com/2013/05/08 /late-term-abortion-doc-caught-comparing-unborn-baby-to-meat-in-a-crock-pot/.
8. "Questions and Answers on Born-Alive Abortion Survivors."
9. "When Does a Fetus Have a Heartbeat?," MedicalNewsToday, last medically reviewed, December 8, 2022, https://www.medicalnewstoday.com/articles/when -does-a-fetus-have-a-heartbeat#timeline.
10. "Senate Judiciary Hearing on Texas Abortion Pill Ruling," C-SPAN, April 26, 2023, https://www.c-span.org/video/?527656-1/senate-judiciary-hearing-texas -abortion-pill-ruling.
11. "Population Growth," Our World in Data, 2022, https://ourworldindata.org /world-population-growth.
12. "Extreme Poverty—Data Documentation," Gapminder, https://www.gapminder .org/data/documentation/epovrate/.
13. Francis Galton, "Eugenics: Its Definition, Scope, and Aims," https://galton.org /essays/1900-1911/galton-1904-am-journ-soc-eugenics-scope-aims.htm.
14. https://galton.org/cgi-bin/searchImages/galton/search/books/human-faculty /pages/galton-human-faculty_0221.htm.
15. "*Buck v Bell*, Superintendent of State Colony Epileptics and Feeble Minded (1927)," Cornell Law School Legal Information Institute, https://www.law.cornell.edu /supremecourt/text/274/200.
16. "Women's Studies and Women's Issues in Vermont: A Research Guide," Smith College Libraries, https://libex.smith.edu/omeka/files/original/d6358bc3053 -c93183295bf2df1c0c931.pdf
17. https://www.britannica.com/topic/American-Birth-Control-League.
18. "Black Abortion Statistics," Right to Life of Michigan, https://rtl.org/multicultural -outreach/black-abortion-statistics/.
19. "Summary of Vital Statistics 2013: Pregnancy Outcomes," New York City Department of Health, https://www.nyc.gov/assets/doh/downloads/pdf/vs/vs -pregnancy-outcomes-2013.pdf.
20. Joseph Ellis, "Bill Gates's Relationship with Jeffrey Epstein Revolved Around One Thing," MSN.com, n.d., https://www.msn.com/en-us/money/companies/bill -gates-s-relationship-with-jeffrey-epstein-revolved-around-one-thing/ar-AA1kDfqZ.
21. Jack Fowler, "Buffett Bequests Billions for Abortion," Philanthropy Daily, July 8, 2022, https://philanthropydaily.com/buffett-bequests-billions-for-abortion/.
22. Hayden Ludwig, "Terror of the Unborn: Billions for Millions of Abortions," Capital Research Center, July 9, 2020, https://capitalresearch.org/article/terror -of-the-unborn-part-1/.
23. Planned Parenthood, https://www.rbf.org/about/our-history/timeline/planned -parenthood.
24. Pam Belluck, "Pregnancy Centers Gain Influence in Anti-Aborton Fight," *The New York Times*, January 4, 2013, https://www.nytimes.com/2013/01/05/health /pregnancy-centers-gain-influence-in-anti-abortion-fight.html.
25. "Fact Sheet: Pregnancy Centers Serving Women and Saving Lives (2020 Study),"

Charlotte Lozier Institute, updated July 2021, https://lozierinstitute.org/fact
-sheet-pregnancy-centers-serving-women-and-saving-lives-2020/.

26. John McCormack, "Cortez Masto Joins Elizabeth Warren's Assault on Crisis
Pregnancy Centers," *National Review*, September 12, 2022, https://www
.nationalreview.com/corner/cortez-masto-joins-elizabeth-warrens-assault-on
-crisis-pregnancy-centers/.

27. Steven Ertelt, "Supreme Court Strikes Down California Law Forcing Pregnancy
Centers to Promote Abortion," LifeNews.com, June 26, 2018, https://www
.lifenews.com/2018/06/26/supreme-court-strikes-down-california-law-forcing
-pregnancy-centers-to-promote-abortion/.

28. Jessica Chasmar, "Over 100 Pro-Life Orgs, Churches Attacked Since Dobbs
Leak," Fox News, October 20, 2022, https://www.foxnews.com/politics/100-pro
-life-orgs-churches-attacked-dobbs-leak.

29. Zaeem Shaikh, "Federal Investigators Looking into Suspicious Fire at Gresham
Pregnancy Center," *The Oregonian*, June 14, 2022, https://www.oregonlive.com
/crime/2022/06/federal-investigators-looking-into-suspicious-fire-at-gresham
-pregnancy-center.html.

30. Houston Keene, "Ohio Pro-Life Pregnancy Center Attacked by Radical 'Jane's
Revenge' Group: 'Abort God,'" Fox News, April 17, 2023, https://www.foxnews
.com/politics/ohio-pro-life-pregnancy-center-attacked-radical-janes-revenge
-abort-god.

31. Larry Celona, Tina Moore, and Amanda Woods, "Graffiti on NYC Church Warns:
'If Abortion Isn't Safe, Neither Are You,'" *New York Post*, June 27, 2022, https://
nypost.com/2022/06/27/janes-revenge-graffitis-nyc-church-with-roe-v-wade
-warnings/.

32. Ben Feuerherd and Gabrielle Fonrouge, "Armed Man Nicholas Roske Arrested
Near Supreme Court Justice Brett Kavanaugh's Home," *New York Post*, June 8,
2022, https://nypost.com/2022/06/08/armed-man-arrested-near-supreme-court
-justice-brett-kavanaughs-home/.

33. Deidre McPhillips, "There Were 32,000 Fewer Legal Abortions in the US in
the Six Months After the Dobbs Decision, New Analysis Suggests," CNN, April
11, 2023, https://www.cnn.com/2023/04/11/health/abortion-decline-post-roe
/index.html.

34. Sam Dorman, "Study: 73 Million Global Abortions Took Place Yearly from
2015–2019," LiveAction, April 13, 2022, https://www.liveaction.org/news/73
-million-global-abortions-yearly/.

35. Willard Cates, Jr., David A. Grimes, and Kenneth F. Schulz, "Public Health Impact of Legal Abortion: 30 Years Later," *Guttmacher Institute* 35, no. 1 (2003),
https://www.guttmacher.org/journals/psrh/2003/01/public-health-impact-legal
-abortion-30-years-later.

36. "5: 'I Regret My Abortion,'" Human Life Alliance, n.d., https://humanlife.org
/5-i-regret-my-abortion.

LIE #2: "Trans Women Are Women"

1. Aleksandr Solzhenitsyn, "Live Not by Lies" Solzhenitsyn Center, February 12,
1974, https://www.solzhenitsyncenter.org/live-not-by-lies.

2. BillboardChris, Twitter post, https://twitter.com/BillboardChris/status/1558823 459651817477?s=20&t=qOqqdGSJ9dLGkkmw0o4XAw.

3. Spencer Lindquist, "NIH Funds Study on Puberty Blockers, Hormones on Youth Despite Risk of Sterilization," Daily Wire, July 10, 2023, https://www.dailywire .com/news/nih-funds-study-on-puberty-blockers-hormones-on-youth-despite-risk -of-sterilization.

4. Aaron Sibarium, "The Hijacking of Pediatric Medicine," The Free Press, December 7, 2022, https://www.thefp.com/p/the-hijacking-of-pediatric-medicine.

5. Fox News, https://www.foxnews.com/video/6307583800112#sp=show-clips.

6. Hannah Grossman, "California School District Sexual Education Curriculum Includes 'Genderbread Identity' Man: 'It's Horrifying,'" Fox News, August 16, 2022, https://www.foxnews.com/media/california-school-district-sexual-education -curriculum-includes-genderbread-identity-man.

7. Christopher F. Rufo, "Radical Gender Lessons for Young Children," City Journal, April 21, 2022, https://www.city-journal.org/article/radical-gender-lessons -for-young-children.

8. Christopher F. Rufo, "How to Combat Gender Theory in Public Schools," City Journal, February 7, 2023, https://www.city-journal.org/article/how-to-combat -gender-theory-in-public-schools.

9. Tyler O'Neil, "Fairfax County Schools Reinstates Books with Explicit Images, Claiming They Don't Include Pedophilia," Fox News, November 24, 2021, https://www.foxnews.com/politics/fairfax-county-schools-reinstates-lawn-boy -genderqueer-claims-pedophilia.

10. Elizabeth Troutman, "School Allows Reading LGBT Book to Second Graders Despite State Law Requiring Parental Consent," Daily Signal, April 27, 2023, https://www.dailysignal.com/2023/04/27/school-allows-reading-lgbt-book -second-graders-despite-state-law-requiring-parental-consent/.

11. Jon Brown, "School Required Us to Lie to Parents About Their Kids' Gender Identity, California Teachers Claim in Lawsuit," Fox News, April 27, 2023, https://www.foxnews.com/us/school-required-us-lie-parents-about-their-kids -gender-identity-california-teachers-claim-lawsuit.

12. Matt Friedman, "New Jersey Sues Three School Districts over Transgender Notification Policy," Politico, June 22, 2023, https://www.politico.com/news/2023 /06/22/murphy-new-jersey-school-districts-transgender-policy-00103127.

13. Tony Kinnett, "California Bill Would Charge Any Parent Who Doesn't Affirm Transgenderism with Child Abuse," Daily Signal, June 9, 2023, https://www .dailysignal.com/2023/06/09/california-bill-would-charge-any-parent-doesnt -affirm-transgenderism-child-abuse/.

14. Emily Matesic, "Middle Schoolers Accused of Sexual Harassment for Not Using Preferred Pronouns, Parents Say," KKTV, May 15, 2022, https://www.kktv .com/2022/05/16/middle-schoolers-accused-sexual-harassment-not-using -preferred-pronouns-parents-say/.

15. "Information on Testosterone Hormone Therapy," University of California, San Francisco, UCSF Transgender Care, July 2020, https://transcare.ucsf.edu/article /information-testosterone-hormone-therapy.

16. C. C. Motosko, G. A. Zakhem, M. K. Pomeranz, and A. Hazen, "Acne: A Side-

Effect of Masculinizing Hormonal Therapy in Transgender Patients," *British Journal of Dermatology* 180, no. 1 (2019): 26–30, doi: 10.1111/bjd.17083.

17. "What Is Erythrocytosis?," WebMD, https://www.webmd.com/a-to-z-guides /what-is-erythrocytosis.

18. M. S. Irwig, "Cardiovascular Health in Transgender People," *Review in Endocrine and Metabolic Disorders* 19, no. 3 (2018): 243–51, doi: 10.1007/s11154 -018-9454-3. PMID: 30073551.

19. J. J. Rasmussen et al., "Endogenous Testosterone Levels Are Associated with Risk of Type 2 Diabetes in Women without Established Comorbidity," *Journal of the Endocrine Society* 4, no. 6 (2020): bvaa050, doi: 10.1210/jendso/bvaa050. PMID: 32537541.

20. Wylie C. Hembree et al., "Endocrine Treatment of Gender-Dysphoric/Gender-Incongruent Persons: An Endocrine Society* Clinical Practice Guideline," *Journal of Clinical Endocrinology & Metabolism* 102, no. 11 (2017): 3869–77 (see Table 10), doi: 10.1210/jc.2017-01962.

21. Nienke M. Nota et al., "Occurrence of Acute Cardiovascular Events in Transgender Individuals Receiving Hormone Therapy," 139, no. 11 (2019): 1461–62.

22. L. J. Seal, "A Review of the Physical and Metabolic Effects of Cross-sex Hormonal Therapy in the Treatment of Gender Dysphoria," *Annals of Clinical Biochemistry* 53, no. 1 (20161): 10–20, doi:10.1177/0004563215587763.

23. D. Getahun, Review of "Cross-Sex Hormones and Acute Cardiovascular Events in Transgender Persons," Healthy Male, September 2018, https://www.healthymale .org.au/research-reviews/cross-sex-hormones-and-acute-cardiovascular-events -transgender-persons

24. Nota et al., "Occurrence of Acute Cardiovascular Events in Transgender Individuals Receiving Hormone Therapy."

25. Richard A. Santucci, "Urethral Complications After Transgender Phalloplasty: Strategies to Treat Them and Minimize Their Occurrence," *Special Issue on the Clinical Anatomy of Transgender Surgery* 31n, no. 2 (2018): 187–90.

26. Alfred C. Kinsey, *Sexual Behavior in the Human Male* (Bloomington and Indianapolis: Indiana University Press, 1948).

27. *Time* cover, August 24, 1953, https://content.time.com/time/covers/0,16641, 19530824,00.html.

28. Dina Spector, "Why Kinsey's Research Remains Even More Controversial Than the 'Masters Of Sex'," *Business Insider*, October 18, 2013, https://www.businessinsider .com/why-alfred-kinsey-was-controversial-2013-10.

29. Anna Slatz, "John Money: The Pro-Pedophile Pervert Who Invented 'Gender,'" Reduxx, January 24, 2022, https://reduxx.info/john-money-the-pervert-who -invented-gender/.

30. Jordan Peterson, "Parental Trauma in a World of Gender Insanity, transcription of the video *Parental Trauma in a World of Gender Insanity*, Miriam Grossman, MD, episode 347," https://www.wisdominanutshell.academy/jordan-b-peterson /parental-trauma-in-a-world-of-gender-insanity-miriam-grossman-md-ep-347 -transcription/.

31. Dr. Miriam Grossman, *Lost in Trans Nation* (New York: Skyhorse Publishing, 2023), 38.

32. James M. Cantor, "American Academy of Pediatrics and Trans-Kids: Fact-Checking Rafferty," JamesCantor.org., 2018, http://www.jamescantor.org/uploads/6/2/9/3/62939641/cantor_fact-check_of_aap.pdf.
33. Undergraduate Student Reference Group Data Report, American College Health Association, 2021, 103, question 67C, https://www.acha.org/documents/ncha/NCHA-III_Spring-2021_Undergraduate_Reference_group_data_report.pdf.
34. Michelle M. Johns et al., "Transgender Identity and Experiences of Violence Victimization, Substance Use, Suicide Risk, and Sexual Risk Behaviors Among High School Students—19 States and Large Urban School Districts, 2017," Centers for Disease Control and Prevention, *Morbidity and Mortality Weekly Report* 68, no. 3 (2019), https://www.cdc.gov/mmwr/volumes/68/wr/mm6803a3.htm.
35. K. M. Kidd et al., "Prevalence of Gender-Diverse Youth in an Urban School District," *Pediatrics* 147, no. 6 (2021): e2020049823, doi: 10.1542/peds.2020-049823.
36. Robin Respaut and Chad Terhune, "Putting Numbers on the Rise in Children Seeking Gender Care," Reuters, https://www.reuters.com/investigates/special-report/usa-transyouth-data/.
37. Respaut and Terhune, "Putting Numbers on the Rise in Children Seeking Gender Care."
38. James Reinl, "California Teen Sues Doctors Over Breast-Removal Surgery at 13 in Kaiser Permanente's Second Blockbuster Trans Lawsuit," Daily Mail, March 17, 2023, https://www.dailymail.co.uk/news/article-11873443/California-teen-sues-doctors-breast-removal-surgery-13-Kaiser-Permanentes-2nd-lawsuit.html.
39. "Affidavit of Jamie Reed," https://ago.mo.gov/wp-content/uploads/2-07-2023-reed-affidavit-signed.pdf, see 31 and 64.
40. Grossman, *Lost in Trans Nation*, 67.
41. Caroline Downey, "Advocate Rather Than a Scientist: The Compromised Research of Child Gender-Transition Doctor Jack Turban," *National Review*, August 16, 2022, https://www.nationalreview.com/news/advocate-rather-than-a-scientist-the-compromised-research-of-child-gender-transition-doctor-jack-turban/.
42. Tiffany Cowen, "Seeking the Truth About Teen Suicides and Puberty Blockers," Women Are Human, February 19, 2020, https://www.womenarehuman.com/seeking-the-truth-about-teen-suicides-and-puberty-blockers/.
43. Jay Greene, Ph.D., "Puberty Blockers, Cross-Sex Hormones, and Youth Suicide," Heritage Foundation, June 13, 2022, https://www.heritage.org/gender/report/puberty-blockers-cross-sex-hormones-and-youth-suicide.
44. L. Littman, "Correction: Parent Reports of Adolescents and Young Adults Perceived to Show Signs of a Rapid Onset of Gender Dysphoria," *PLOS ONE* 14, no. 3 (2019): e0214157, https://www.ncbi.nlm.nih.gov/pmc/articles/PMC6424391.
45. Littman, "Correction: Parent Reports of Adolescents and Young Adults Perceived to Show Signs of a Rapid Onset of Gender Dysphoria."
46. Lifehacker, "What Pornhub's 2021 Search Trends Say About Us," https://lifehacker.com/what-pornhubs-2021-search-trends-say-about-us-1848412206.
47. "NYC Trans Oral History Project: Transcript: Andrea Long Chu," November 2, 2018, https://nyctransoralhistory.org/content/uploads/2021/11/NYC-TOHP-Transcript-107-Andrea-Long-Chu_UPDATED.pdf.
48. SRS Market Analysis, 2021, Grand View Research, https://acrobat.adobe.com

/link/review?uri=urn%3Aaaid%3Ascds%3AUS%3A8a5b2d8b-4621-48a3-be7d
-ade550dfb109.

49. Amanda Prestigiacomo, "How the Vanderbilt Gender Surgery Scandal Only
Leads to More Questions," Daily Wire, n.d., https://www.dailywire.com/news
/how-the-vanderbilt-gender-surgery-scandal-only-leads-to-more-questions.

50. Joe Bukuras, "Tennessee Governor Urges Investigation of Vanderbilt Pediatric
Transgender Clinic," *National Catholic Register*, September 22, 2022, https://
www.ncregister.com/cna/tennessee-governor-urges-investigation-of-vanderbilt
-pediatric-transgender-clinic.

51. "Transgender Health Care: Does Health Insurance Cover Gender-Affirming
Surgery?"

52. Susan Berry, "Vanderbilt's Gender Clinic Doctor: Trans Surgeries 'Make Money
for the Hospital,'" *Tennessee Star*, September 21, 2022, https://tennesseestar.com
/the-tennessee-star/vanderbilts-gender-clinic-doctor-trans-surgeries-make-money
-for-the-hospital/sberry/2022/09/21/.

53. James Gordon, "Trans Woman Cyclist Wins North Carolina Race by Crossing
Finish Line FIVE MINUTES Ahead of Runner-Up," *Daily Mail*, June 12, 2023,
https://www.dailymail.co.uk/news/article-12184553/Trans-cyclist-wins-North
-Carolina-women-race-crossing-finish-line-FIVE-MINUTES-ahead-runner-up
.html.

54. Ian Shutts, "After Being TKO'd by Fallon Fox, Tamikka Brents Says Transgender
Fighters in MMA 'Just Isn't Fair,'" LowKick MMA, April 19, 2017, https://
www.lowkickmma.com/after-being-tkod-by-fallon-fox-tamikka-brents-says
-transgender-fighters-in-mma-just-isnt-fair/.

55. Zachary Evans, "Female Inmate Claims She Was Raped by Transgender Inmate
Who Was Placed in Illinois Women's Prison," *National Review*, February 21,
2020, https://www.nationalreview.com/news/female-inmate-claims-she-was-raped
-by-transgender-inmate-who-was-placed-in-illinois-womens-prison/.

56. Alex Hammer, "Transgender 'pervert' is arrested 15 months after she 'exposed
herself to women and girls at Wi Spa in LA' triggering violent protests from An-
tifa goons who branded allegations a bigoted hoax," Daily Mail, December 19,
2022, https://www.dailymail.co.uk/news/article-11555915/Transgender-pervert
-arrested-15-months-exposed-women-Wi-Spa-LA.html.

57. Jon Brown, "Trans Woman Crawled into Bed with, Assaulted Female Resident at
Women's Shelter: Police," Fox News, April 20, 2023, https://www.foxnews
.com/world/trans-woman-crawled-bed-assaulted-female-resident-womens
-shelter-police.

58. Preston Sprinkle, "Should Christians Use Preferred Pronouns?" YouTube, 10:32,
THINKQ Media, May 22, 2022, https://www.youtube.com/watch?v=onj7o
-VLCb8.

LIE #3: "Love Is Love"

1. Izz Scott LaMagdeleine, "Did Biden Say in 2006 That 'Marriage Is Between a
Man and a Woman'?," Snopes, June 25, 2023, https://www.snopes.com/fact-check
/biden-gay-marriage-2006/.

2. "More Support for Gun Rights, Gay Marriage Than in 2008 or 2004," Pew

Research Center, April 25, 2012, https://www.pewresearch.org/politics/2012/04/25/more-support-for-gun-rights-gay-marriage-than-in-2008-or-2004/.

3. "1996 Defense of Marriage Act (DOMA)," William J. Clinton Presidential Library & Museum, https://clinton.presidentiallibraries.us/collections/show/86.

4. https://www.youtube.com/watch?v=qlgkDCZI1CQ.

5. "Why Family Matters: Comprehensive Analysis of the Consequences of Family Breakdown," Centre for Social Justice, March 2019, https://www.centrefor socialjustice.org.uk/library/why-family-matters-comprehensive-analysis-of-the -consequences-of-family-breakdown.

6. Brad Wilcox and Hal Boyd, "The Nuclear Family Is Still Dispensable," February 21, 2020, *The Atlantic*, https://www.theatlantic.com/ideas/archive/2020/02/nuclear-family-still-indispensable/606841/.

7. Alexandra Thompson and Susannah N. Tapp, "Just the Stats Violent Victimization by Race or Hispanic Origin, 2008–2021," Bureau of Justice Statistics, July 2023, https://bjs.ojp.gov/violent-victimization-race-or-hispanic-origin-2008-2021.

8. Martin et al., Center for Disease Control and Prevention, National Vital Statistics Reports, "Births: Final Data for 2018," vol. 68, no. 13, https://www.cdc.gov/nchs/data/nvsr/nvsr68/nvsr68_13_tables-508.pdf.

9. Martin et al., Center for Disease Control and Prevention, National Vital Statistics Reports, "Births: Final Data for 2018."

10. Robert Hart, "Kids Raised by Same-Sex Parents Fare Same As—Or Better Than— Kids of Straight Couples, Research Finds," March 6, 2023, *Forbes*, https://www.forbes.com/sites/roberthart/2023/03/06/kids-raised-by-same-sex-parents-fare -same-as-or-better-than-kids-of-straight-couples-research-finds/?sh=7693dc 797738.

11. https://pubmed.ncbi.nlm.nih.gov/23017845/; https://onlinelibrary.wiley.com/doi/10.1111/j.1741-3737.2012.00966.x; https://pubmed.ncbi.nlm.nih.gov/19631107/; https://pubmed.ncbi.nlm.nih.gov/18194035/; https://www.cam bridge.org/core/journals/children-australia/article/abs/children-in-three -contexts-family-education-and-social-development/BA0DB5DC62B9E7D 955454A5BB165F7F8; https://link.springer.com/article/10.1007/s11150-013 -9220-y; https://gh.bmj.com/content/bmjgh/8/3/e010556.full.pdf?with-ds =yes.

12. Maressa Brown, "Lance Bass says it was 'hard not to get discouraged' during his 'difficult' surrogacy journey: 'Am I being told that I should not have kids?'" Yahoo Life, May 28, 2023, https://www.yahoo.com/lifestyle/lance-bass-twins-ivf -surrogacy-challenges-144548443.html#:~:text=%E2%80%9CIt's%20just %20the%20best%2C%20warmest,do%20that%20with%20my%20mom.

13. https://www.huffpost.com/entry/i-love-gay-people-and-christians_b_3497785

14. Rosaria Butterfield, "Love Your Neighbor Enough to Speak Truth," Gospel Co-alition, October 31, 2016, https://www.thegospelcoalition.org/article/love-your -neighbor-enough-to-speak-truth/.

15. "Masterpiece Cakeshop v. Colorado Civil Rights Commission," Alliance Defending Freedom, n.d., https://adflegal.org/case/masterpiece-cakeshop-v-colorado -civil-rights-commission.

16. "Jack Phillips," Alliance Defending Freedom, n.d., https://adflegal.org/client /jack-phillips.

17. "Activist Lawyer Targets Jack Phillips in Third Lawsuit," Alliance Defending Freedom, https://adflegal.org/article/activist-lawyer-targets-jack-phillips-third -lawsuit.

LIE #4: "No Human Is Illegal"

1. C. S. Lewis, *The Four Loves* (New York: Harper One, 1960, 2017).
2. Samantha Schmidt, "A Noncriminal Mother of Four Was Deported. Now in Mexico, She Fears for Her Safety," *The Washington Post*, April 28, 2017, https:// www.washingtonpost.com/news/morning-mix/wp/2017/04/28/a-non-criminal -mother-of-four-was-deported-now-in-mexico-she-fears-for-her-safety/.
3. Ray Sanchez, "San Francisco Death: Kate Steinle's Family Files Lawsuit," CNN, May 28, 2016, https://www.cnn.com/2016/05/27/us/kate-steinle-wrongful -death-suit/index.html.
4. Holly Yan and Dan Simon, "Undocumented immigrant acquitted in Kate Steinle death," CNN, December 1, 2017, https://www.cnn.com/2017/11/30/us/kate -steinle-murder-trial-verdict/index.html.
5. Yaron Steinbuch, "Illegal Immigrant Faces Life After Beheading Girlfriend with a Machete Inside Car in Minnesota," *New York Post*, May 15, 2023, https://nypost .com/2023/05/15/illegal-immigrant-convicted-of-murder-for-beheading -girlfriend/.
6. Paul Blume and Katie Wermus, "Shakopee Decapitation Killer Deemed Not Guilty, Mentally Ill," Fox 9 KMSP, https://www.fox9.com/news/shakopee-decapitation -killer-deemed-not-guilty-mentally-ill.
7. "Criminal Noncitizen Statistics, Fiscal Years 2017–2024," U.S. Customs and Bor- der Protection, https://www.cbp.gov/newsroom/stats/cbp-enforcement-statistics /criminal-noncitizen-statistics.
8. Joel Rose, "Border Patrol Apprehensions Hit a Record High. But That's Only Part of the Story," NPR, October 23, 2021, https://www.npr.org/2021/10/23 /1048522086/border-patrol-apprehensions-hit-a-record-high-but-thats-only -part-of-the-story.
9. Infoplease staff, "Top 50 Cities in the U.S. by Population & Rank," Infoplease, updated July 21, 2023, https://www.infoplease.com/us/cities/top-50-cities-us -population-and-rank.
10. "U.S. States—Ranked by Population 2024," World Population Review, https:// worldpopulationreview.com/states.
11. Rose, "Border Patrol Apprehensions."
12. "U.S. States—Ranked by Population 2024."
13. Jeffrey S. Passel and Jens Manuel Krogstad, "What We Know About Unautho- rized Immigrants Living in the US," Pew Research Center, November 16, 2023, https://www.pewresearch.org/short-reads/2023/11/16/what-we-know-about -unauthorized-immigrants-living-in-the-us/#:~:text=The%20unauthorized %20immigrant%20population%20in,of%2012.2%20million%20in%202007.
14. Julia Ainsley, "Number of People on Terrorist Watchlist Stopped at Southern U.S. Border Has Risen," NBC News, September 14, 2023, https://www.nbcnews.com /politics/national-security/number-people-terror-watchlist-stopped-mexico -us-border-risen-rcna105095.

15. "Agent Staffing of the U.S. Border Patrol from FY 1992 to 2020," Statista, November 3, 2023, https://www.statista.com/statistics/455866/us-border-patrol -agent-staffing/.
16. Stephen Dinan, "MS-13's Wave of Murder Fueled by Illegal Immigrants," *Washington Times*, October 22, 2020, https://www.washingtontimes.com/news/2020 /oct/22/ms-13s-wave-murder-fueled-illegal-immigrant/.
17. Daniel Horowitz, "Texas Town Overrun with Crime and Disease: The Mayor Has Had Enough," Blaze Media, June 11, 2019, https://www.theblaze.com/columns /opinion/texas-town-overrun-with-crime-and-disease-the-mayor-has-had-enough.
18. Bob Price, "Exclusive Video: Border Crisis Disrupts Texas Ranchers' Lives 'Worse Than Ever,' Says Governor," Breitbart, March 14, 2022, https://www .breitbart.com/border/2022/03/14/exclusive-video-border-crisis-disrupts -texas-ranchers-lives-worse-than-ever-says-governor/.
19. Julia Tomascik, "Texas Ranchers Testify Before House, Senate on Border Security," Texas Farm Bureau, March 23, 2023, https://texasfarmbureau.org/texas-ranchers -testify-before-house-senate-on-border-security/.
20. Vanda Felbab-Brown, "China's Role in the Fentanyl Crisis," Brookings Institution, March 31, 2023, https://www.brookings.edu/articles/chinas-role-in-the -fentanyl-crisis/.
21. "Are Fentanyl Overdose Deaths Rising in the US?," USAFacts, September 27, 2023, https://usafacts.org/articles/are-fentanyl-overdose-deaths-rising-in-the-us /#footnote-source-1.
22. Julia Bingel, "Akron 2-Year-Old Dies from Fentanyl Overdose, Officials Say," Cleveland 19 News, January 30, 2023, https://www.cleveland19.com/2023/01 /30/akron-2-year-old-dies-fentanyl-overdose-officials-say/.
23. Associated Press, "1-Year-Old Dies from Fentanyl Overdose in Baton Rouge," *U.S. News & World Report*, November 4, 2022, https://www.usnews.com/news /best-states/louisiana/articles/2022-11-04/1-year-old-dies-from-fentanyl -overdose-in-baton-rouge.
24. Luz Pena, "'A shock': Parent speaks after 10-month-old survives fentanyl overdose at SF park," ABC News, December 1, 2022, https://abc7news.com/baby-fentanyl -overdose-sf-moscone-park-playground-accidental-drug-san-francisco-drugs /12516644.
25. George J. Borjas, "Who's to Blame for the Economy? Trump, Clinton and Immigration," *Politico Magazine*, September–October 2016, https://www.politico .com/magazine/story/2016/09/trump-clinton-immigration-economy -unemployment-jobs-214216/.
26. Wesley Hunt, Twitter post, September 27, 2023, 8:05 A.M., @WesleyHuntTX, https://twitter.com/wesleyhunttx/status/1707018640153776425.

"Veteran Frank Tammaro, a 95-year-old Korean War veteran said he was given less than two months' notice to figure out where he was going to live after the nursing home he resided in was sold to become a facility for undocumented migrants. 'The thing I'm annoyed about is how they did it, it was very disgraceful what they did to the people in Island Shores,' Tammaro said, referencing the assisted living facility he was in. 'Then one day there was a notice on the board. I think that gave us a month and a half to find out where we were going to go,' he said. 'I thought my suitcases were going to be on the curb because I'm not that fast,' said Tammaro. New York City Councilman David Carr confirmed to local outlet SI Live that he was informed by the city's Department of Social Services that the migrant facility would open there this week. Where are our priorities in this country when military veterans, our heroes, are being evicted to make room for Joe Biden's handpicked illegal aliens? And this is what we're being asked to continue to fund, the invasion of our sovereign border? The eviction of our greatest Americans in exchange for criminal aliens? Enough."

27. Editorial, "Hillary Clinton's 'Illegal' Flip-Flop," *New York Post*, November 29, 2015, https://nypost.com/2015/11/29/hillary-clintons-illegal-flip-flop/.
28. John Wagner, "Trump Touted Obama's 2005 Remarks on Immigration. Here's What Obama Actually Said," *The Washington Post*, October 24, 2018, https://www.washingtonpost.com/politics/trump-touted-obamas-2005-remarks-on-immigration-heres-what-obama-actually-said/2018/10/24/1ed845c0-d782-11e8-aeb7-ddcad4a0a54e_story.html.
29. Andrew Kaczynski, "Joe Biden Once Said A Fence Was Needed to Stop 'Tons' of Drugs from Mexico," CNN, May 10, 2019, https://www.cnn.com/2019/05/10/politics/kfile-biden-drugs-fence-2006/index.html.
30. Muzaffar Chishti, Sarah Pierce, and Jessica Bolter, "The Obama Record on Deportations: Deporter in Chief or Not?," Migration Policy Institute, January 26, 2017, https://www.migrationpolicy.org/article/obama-record-deportations-deporter-chief-or-not.
31. Michael D. Shear and Spencer S. Hsu, "Emanuel Says Immigration Reform Bill Lacks Votes to Pass," *The Washington Post*, June 25, 2009, https://www.washingtonpost.com/wp-dyn/content/article/2009/06/25/AR2009062501914_2.html?hpid=moreheadlines.
32. Lukas Mikelionis, "AOC's Office Denies Claims That Photos Near Migrant Detention Center Were Staged," Fox News, June 27, 2019, https://www.foxnews.com/politics/ocasio-cortez-mocked-staged-emotional-photoshoot-detention-facility.
33. Domenico Montanaro, "Democratic Candidates Call Trump a White Supremacist, a Label Some Say Is 'Too Simple,'" NPR, August 15, 2019, https://www.npr.org/2019/08/15/751215391/democratic-candidates-call-trump-a-white-supremacist-a-label-some-say-is-too-sim.
34. Alyssa Milano, Twitter post, Jan 10, 2019, 3:48 P.M., @Alyssa_Milano, https://twitter.com/Alyssa_Milano/status/1083465553300185088?ref_src=twsrc%5Etfw%7Ctwcamp%5Etweetembed%7Ctwterm%5E1083465553300185088%7Ctwgr%5Ece76a4ce75981968b477a69bed186aa190f2af91%7Ctwcon%5Esl_c10&ref_url=https%3A%2F%2Fwww.lifezette.com%2F2019%2F01%2Falyssa-milano-calls-proposed-border-wall-trumps-symbol-to-white-supremacy%2F.
35. Jose A. DelReal, "This Time, Hillary Clinton Supports Giving Driver's Licenses to Undocumented Immigrants," *The Washington Post*, April 16, 2015, https://www.washingtonpost.com/news/post-politics/wp/2015/04/16/this-time-hillary-clinton-supports-giving-drivers-licenses-to-undocumented-immigrants/.
36. "Remarks by the President in Address to the Nation on Immigration," Obama White House Archives, November 20, 2014, https://obamawhitehouse.archives.gov/the-press-office/2014/11/20/remarks-President-address-nation-immigration.
37. Myah Ward, "Biden Campaign Slams 'Extreme' and 'Racist' Trump Immigration Plans," *Politico*, November 11, 2023, https://www.politico.com/news/2023/11

/11/biden-campaign-slams-extreme-and-racist-trump-immigration-plans-00126712.

38. Mike Huckabee, "National View: Flip-Flop—The Inconvenient Truth About Dems' History on the Wall," *Duluth News Tribune*, January 13, 2019, https://www.duluthnewstribune.com/opinion/national-view-flip-flop-the-inconvenient-truth-about-dems-history-on-the-wall.

39. Christopher Hickey et al., "Here Are the Executive Actions Biden Signed in His First 100 Days," CNN, updated April 30, 2021, https://www.cnn.com/interactive/2021/politics/biden-executive-orders/.

40. Lawrence Hurley, "Biden administration asks Supreme Court to allow Border Patrol to cut or move razor wire at Texas border," NBC News, January 2, 2024, https://www.nbcnews.com/politics/supreme-court/biden-administration-asks-supreme-court-allow-border-patrol-cut-move-r-rcna131964.

41. Todd Bensman, "Government Admission: Biden Parole Flights Create Security 'Vulnerabilities' at U.S. Airports," Center for Immigration Studies, March 4 2024, https://cis.org/Bensman/Government-Admission-Biden-Parole-Flights-Create-Security-Vulnerabilities-US-Airports.

42. Michael Lee, "Migrants in Potentially the Largest Caravan Ever Demands Biden Keep Asylum Promise," Fox News, June 6, 2022, https://www.foxnews.com/world/immigrant-largest-caravan-biden-promise-asylum.

43. Laura Gottesdiener, "Biden Tells Migrants to Stay Put. Central Americans Hear a Different Message," Reuters, March 31, 2021, https://www.reuters.com/article/us-usa-immigration-messaging-insight/biden-tells-immigrants-to-stay-put-central-americans-hear-a-different-message-idUSKBN2BN1BB/.

44. Lydia Saad, "Americans Still Value Immigration, but Have Concerns," Gallup, July 13, 2023, https://news.gallup.com/poll/508520/americans-value-immigration-concerns.aspx.

45. Public Opinon/Immigration, "On immigration, most buying into idea of "invasion" at southern border," Ipsos, August 28, 2022, https://www.ipsos.com/en-us/news-polls/npr-immigration-perceptions-august-2022.

46. Rafael Bernal, "Biden Stuns Allies with Border Wall Bombshell," *The Hill*, October 6, 2023, https://thehill.com/latino/4241165-bidens-border-wall-bombshell-shocks-allies/.

47. Mirna Alsharif and Erick Mendoza, "Infant and Toddler Found Alone in Arizona Desert," NBC News, August 27, 2022, https://www.nbcnews.com/news/us-news/infant-toddler-found-alone-arizona-desert-rcna45103.

48. Stef W. Kight, "Inside a Family's Harrowing Journey to the U.S. Border," Axios, May 12, 2023, https://www.axios.com/2023/05/12/inside-migrant-family-journey-us-mexico-border.

49. José Ignacio Castañeda Perez, "'Boom of Opportunities': How Smugglers, Mexican Cartels Profit from US Border Restrictions," azcentral, updated December 27, 2022, https://www.azcentral.com/in-depth/news/politics/border-issues/2022/12/16/how-cartels-profit-immigrants-desperation-along-u-s-mexico-border/10704315002/.

50. Jude Joffe-Block, "Women Crossing the U.S. Border Face Sexual Assault with Little Protection," *PBS NewsHour*, March 31, 2014, https://www.pbs.org/newshour/nation/facing-risk-rape-migrant-women-prepare-birth-control.

51. Jude Joffe-Block, "Facing the Risk of Rape, Immigrant Women Prepare with Birth Control," *PBS NewsHour*, March 31, 2024, https://www.pbs.org/newshour/nation/facing-risk-rape-migrant-women-prepare-birth-control.

52. "Forced to Flee: Central America's Northern Triangle," Doctors Without Borders, May 2017, https://www.doctorswithoutborders.org/sites/default/files/2018-06/msf_forced-to-flee-central-americas-northern-triangle.pdf.

53. Joffe-Block, "Women Crossing the U.S. Border."

54. "Risk Map 2023 Analysis: Mexico Cartel War," Global Guardian, October 10, 2022, https://www.globalguardian.com/newsroom/risk-map-mexico.

55. Miriam Jordan, "Smuggling Migrant at the Border Now a Billion-Dollar Business," *The New York Times*, July 25, 2022, https://www.nytimes.com/2022/07/25/us/migrant-smuggling-evolution.html.

56. "Mission and impact of the ILO," International Labour Organization, https://www.ilo.org/global/about-the-ilo/mission-and-objectives/features/WCMS_652510/lang--en/index.htm.

57. Elliott Davis Jr., "10 OECD Countries with the Most Migrants," *U.S. News and World Report*, February 21, 2024, https://www.usnews.com/news/best-countries/slideshows/10-countries-that-take-the-most-immigrants.

58. Jeanen Batalova, "Frequently Requested Statistics on Immigrants and Immigration in the United States," Migration Policy Institute, March 13, 2024, https://www.migrationpolicy.org/article/frequently-requested-statistics-immigrants-and-immigration-united-states.

59. Nick Routley, "Countries with the Highest (and Lowest) Proportion of Immigrants," Visual Capitalist, November 22, 2022, https://www.visualcapitalist.com/countries-with-the-highest-proportion-of-immigrants/.

60. Rick Noack, "Leaked Document Says 2,000 Men Allegedly Assaulted 1,200 German Women on New Year's Eve," *The Washington Post*, July 11, 2016, https://www.washingtonpost.com/news/worldviews/wp/2016/07/10/leaked-document-says-2000-men-allegedly-assaulted-1200-german-women-on-new-years-eve.

61. Justin Huggler, "Teenager 'Raped and Left Pregnant' in Cologne Attacks," *The Telegraph*, July 15, 2016, https://www.telegraph.co.uk/news/2016/07/15/teenager-became-pregnant-after-cologne-sex-attacks/.

62. Charlie Duxbury, "Sweden's New Normal: Bombs in the Suburbs on a Weeknight," *Politico*, October 3, 2023, https://www.politico.eu/article/sweden-new-normal-bomb-attacks-suburbs-kristersson-elections-2024/.

63. "Swedish PM Says Integration of Immigrants Has Failed, Fueled Gang Crime," Reuters, April 28, 2022, https://www.reuters.com/world/europe/swedish-pm-says-integration-immigrants-has-failed-fueled-gang-crime-2022-04-28.

64. Bob D'Angelo, "Hamas Attacks: Israeli, Palestinian Backers Hold Rallies Across U.S.," Boston 25News, October 8, 2023, https://www.boston25news.com/news/trending/hamas-attack-israeli-palestinian-backers-hold-rallies-across-us/REEXIGLAZRBAFOPPDSWRWTVI2U/.

65. Lewis, *The Four Loves.*

66. https://www.gutenberg.org/files/27250/27250-h/27250-h.htm.

67. Samuel Smith, "On Immigration, Some Evangelicals Mistake 'America for the Kingdom of God': Former Muslim Pastor," Christian Post, January 21, 2019,

https://www.christianpost.com/news/on-immigration-some-evangelicals
-mistake-america-for-the-kingdom-of-god-former-muslim-pastor.html.

68. Elizabeth Dias, "Donald Trump's Feud with Evangelical Leader Reveals Fault
Lines," *Time*, May 9, 2016, https://time.com/4323009/donald-trump-southern
-baptist-russell-moore-evangelicals-christianity/.

69. Kate Shellnutt, "Evangelicals to Trump: Don't Deport Our Next Generation
of Church Leaders," Christianity Today, September 1, 2017, https://www
.christianitytoday.com/news/2017/september/evangelicals-to-trump-dont-deport
-dreamers-daca-immigration.html.

70. Matthew Soerens and Daniel Darling, "The Gospel and Immigration," The Gospel
Coalition, May 1, 2012, https://www.thegospelcoalition.org/article/the-gospel
-and-immigration/.

71. The Dissenter, Twitter post, September 26, 2023, 1:18 P.M., @Disntr, https://
twitter.com/disntr/status/1706735070642405442, "David Platt says he's
'troubled' by the fact that Christians are resistant to mass influx of 'refugees'
(leftist code word for 'illegal aliens') in our country, despite the fact that it desta-
bilizes society and will ultimately harm the 'missions' he advocates for in the long
run."

72. "Refugees and Asylees Annual Flow Report," U.S. Department of Homeland
Security, https://www.dhs.gov/ohss/topics/immigration/refugees-asylees-afr#:~:
text=A%20refugee%20is%20a%20person,social%20group%2C%20or%20political
%20opinion.

LIE #5: "Social Justice Is Justice"

1. Maria Cramer, "3 Officers Fired Over Photos Taken Near Elijah McClain Memo-
rial, *The New York Times*, July 4, 2020, https://www.nytimes.com/2020/07/04
/us/Elijah-McClain-aurora-police-officers.html.

2. "Social Justice in an Open World," United Nations, 2006, https://www.un.org
/esa/socdev/documents/ifsd/SocialJustice.pdf.

3. ElizabethPrata, Twitter post, November 13, 2023, 5:48 A.M., @ElizabethPrata,
https://twitter.com/elizabethprata/status/1724016415751966905.

4. Woke Preacher Clips, Twitter post, August 25, 2020, 6:39 P.M., @WokePreacherTV,
https://twitter.com/wokepreachertv/status/1298889538100973569.

5. "#DefundThePolice," Black Lives Matter, May 30, 2020, https://blacklivesmatter
.com/defundthepolice/.

6. Mariame Kaba, "Opinion: Yes, We Mean Literally Abolish the Police," *The New
York Times*, June 12, 2020, https://www.nytimes.com/2020/06/12/opinion
/sunday/floyd-abolish-defund-police.html.

7. Zusha Elinson, Dan Frosch, and Joshua Jamerson, "Cities Reverse Defunding
the Police Amid Rising Crime," *The Wall Street Journal*, May 26, 2021, https://
www.wsj.com/articles/cities-reverse-defunding-the-police-amid-rising-crime
-11622066307.

8. Heather Gillers and Andrea Fuller, "Cities Weigh Cutting Police Budgets and
Discover How Hard That Is," *The Wall Street Journal*, August 12, 2020, https://
www.wsj.com/articles/cities-weigh-cutting-police-budgets-and-discover-how-hard
-that-is-11597261079?mod=searchresults&page=1&pos=1&mod=article_inline.

9. "Yahoo! News Race and Justice Survey—May 31, 2020," YouGov.com, https:// docs.cdn.yougov.com/098uixfv4a/20200531_yahoo_race_and_justice_toplines .pdf.

10. Elinson, Frosch, and Jamerson, "Cities Reverse Defunding the Police."

11. Heather Knight, "After Death of Baby, S.F. Domestic Violence Victim Advocates Ask Whether Chesa Boudin Is Doing Enough," *San Francisco Chronicle*, updated April 24, 2021, https://www.sfchronicle.com/local/heatherknight/article /After-death-of-baby-S-F-domestic-violence-16125362.php.

12. Max Rivera et al., "Teen Tourists Stabbed by Deranged Stranger at Grand Central Who Shouted 'I Want All the White People Dead' on Christmas: Police," *New York Post*, December 26, 2023, https://nypost.com/2023/12/26/metro /two-girls-14-and-16-stabbed-at-grand-central-on-christmas/.

13. Rebecca Rosenberg, "Waukesha Suspect Darrell Brooks Allegedly Ran Over Ex-Girlfriend with SUV After Catching Her with Another Man," Fox News, December 2, 2021, https://www.foxnews.com/us/darrell-brooks-allegedly-ran-over-ex -girlfriend-with-suv-catching-her-another-man.

14. Greg B. Smith and Suhail Baht, "Half of Bail Reform Release Program Participants Rearrested, State Stats Show," licpost, January 10, 2022, https://licpost.com /half-of-bail-reform-release-program-participants-rearrested-state-stats-show.

15. Julio Rosas, *Fiery (but Mostly Peaceful): The 2020 Riots and the Gaslighting of America* (Nashville, TN: Daily Wire Books, 2022).

16. "Inmate Race," Federal Bureau of Prisons, April 13, 2024, https://www.bop .gov/about/statistics/statistics_inmate_race.jsp.

17. "Table 43: Arrests by Race and Ethnicity, 2019," FBI, 2019: Crime in the United States, https://ucr.fbi.gov/crime-in-the-u.s/2019/crime-in-the-u.s.-2019/topic -pages/tables/table-43.

18. Curtis Bunn, "Report: Black People Are Still Killed by Police at a Higher Rate Than Other Groups," NBC News, March 3, 2022, https://www.nbcnews.com /news/nbcblk/report-black-people-are-still-killed-police-higher-rate-groups -rcna17169

19. https://ucr.fbi.gov/leoka/2014/tables/table_47_leos_fk_race_and_sex_of _known_offender_2005-2014.xls; https://www.politifact.com/factchecks/2009 /jul/28/bill-bennett/black-men-are-4-percent-americans-35-percent-murde/

20. chrome-extension://efaidnbmnnnibpcajpcglclefindmkaj/https://scholar.harvard .edu/files/fryer/files/empirical_analysis_tables_figures.pdf.

21. Kevin McCaffree, PhD, and Anondah Saide, PhD, "How Informed are Americans about Race and Policing?" Skeptic Research Center, February 20, 2021, https:// www.skeptic.com/research-center/reports/Research-Report-CUPES-007.pdf.

22. Hayden Godfrey et al., *Washington Post*, updated June 10, 2024, https://www .washingtonpost.com/graphics/investigations/police-shootings-database/

23. Heather Mac Donald, *When Race Trumps Merit* (Nashville, TN: Daily Wire Books, 2023), 234.

24. Toluse Olorunnipa and Griff Witte, "George Floyd's America: Born with Two Strikes," *The Washington Post*, October 8, 2023, https://www.washingtonpost.com /graphics/2020/national/george-floyd-america/systemic-racism/.

25. Carlos Ballesteros and Adam Mahoney, "Kenosha Police Shooting of Jacob Blake Spotlights Systemic Racism, Police Spending in Wisconsin," Injustice Watch, August

31, 2020, https://www.injusticewatch.org/news/2020/kenosha-police-funding-racism-jacob-blake/.

26. Eric Levenson and Erica Henry, "Rayshard Brooks Remembered as a Hardworking Father Kept Down by a Racist Legal System," CNN, June 23, 2020, https://www.cnn.com/2020/06/23/us/rayshard-brooks-funeral/index.html.

27. "Black Lives Matter Global Network Responds After Wisconsin District Attorney Won't Charge Kenosha Police Officer in Jacob Blake Shooting," Black Lives Matter Global Network, January 5, 2021, https://blacklivesmatter.com/black-lives-matter-global-network-responds-after-wisconsin-district-attorney-wont-charge-kenosha-police-officer-in-jacob-blake-shooting/.

28. Shaun King, "Atlanta Police Shot and Killed Rayshard Brooks . . ." Facebook post, June 13, 2020, https://www.facebook.com/shaunking/posts/atlanta-police-shot-and-killed-rayshard-brooks-after-they-confronted-him-when-wa/3231850170187212/.

29. https://www.youtube.com/watch?v=kCNKv_7W9a8.

30. "B02001. RACE—Universe: Total population," American Community Survey 1-Year Estimates, 2021, U.S. Census Bureau, https://data.census.gov/table/ACSST1Y2021.S1501.

31. "B19013D: MEDIAN HOUSEHOLD INCOME IN THE PAST 12 MONTHS (IN 2021 INFLATION-ADJUSTED DOLLARS) (ASIAN ALONE HOUSEHOLDER)," American Community Survey 1-Year Estimates, 2021, U.S. Census Bureau, https://data.census.gov/table/ACSST1Y2022.S1901.

32. Bloomberg, "Corporate America Promised to Hire a Lot More People of Color. It Actually Did." updated September 26, 2023, https://www.bloomberg.com/graphics/2023-black-lives-matter-equal-opportunity-corporate-diversity/.

33. Jon Jeter, "Mugabe Vilifies White Farmers," Washington Post, April 19, 2000, https://www.washingtonpost.com/archive/politics/2000/04/19/mugabe-vilifies-white-farmers/14aa4f36-d286-40b2-b617-ca7377d82a09/.

34. "Zimbabwe's Robert Mugabe 'Left $10m but No Will,'" BBC, December 3, 2019, https://www.bbc.com/news/world-africa-50641967.